DESIGNED FOR THE FUTURE

DESIGNED
FOR THE
FUTURE

---

80 PRACTICAL IDEAS FOR A SUSTAINABLE WORLD

Jared Green

PRINCETON ARCHITECTURAL PRESS · NEW YORK

Published by
Princeton Architectural Press
37 East Seventh Street
New York, New York 10003

Visit our website at www.papress.com

Editor: Meredith Baber
Designers: Mia Johnson and Paul Wagner

Special thanks to: Sara Bader, Nicola Bednarek Brower, Janet Behning, Erin Cain,
Megan Carey, Carina Cha, Andrea Chlad, Tom Cho, Barbara Darko, Benjamin English,
Russell Fernandez, Jan Cigliano Hartman, Jan Haux, Diane Levinson, Jennifer Lippert,
Emily Malinowski, Katharine Myers, Jaime Nelson, Rob Shaeffer, Sara Stemen,
Marielle Suba, Kaymar Thomas, Joseph Weston, and Janet Wong
of Princeton Architectural Press —Kevin C. Lippert, publisher

Library of Congress Cataloging-in-Publication Data
Designed for the future : 80 practical ideas for a sustainable world /
[edited by] Jared Green.
    pages   cm
ISBN 978-1-61689-300-2 (paperback)
1. Sustainable design. 2. Sustainable architecture. I. Green, Jared, 1975– editor.
NK1520.D4665 2014
745.401'12—DC23
                                                                2014034253

CONTENTS

9   INTRODUCTION: WHAT GIVES YOU HOPE FOR THE FUTURE?

14   **ABOMEY** SUZANNE PRESTON BLIER

16   **ACEQUIAS** MAKANI THEMBA

18   **ANGKOR WAT** RICK COOK

20   **ANN DEMEULEMEESTER SHOP** MARC KUSHNER

22   **LAS ARBOLEDAS** MARIA BELLALTA

24   **ARTISTS FOR HUMANITY** JASON SCHUPBACH

26   **BEDZED** JEMMA GREEN

28   **BEFORE I DIE** PAUL FARMER

30   **BIOMIMICRY AND BIODESIGN** BLAINE BROWNELL

32   **BRADDOCK, PENNSYLVANIA** THOMAS WOLTZ

34   **THE BRITISH AMBASSADOR'S RESIDENCE** LEO A. DALY III

36   **BUCKMINSTER FULLER'S DYMAXION MAP** MARIA AIOLOVA

38   **THE BURNHAM PLAN** TERESA CÓRDOVA

40   **BUTARO HOSPITAL** JOHN CARY

42   **CALW** CHRISTIAN GABRIEL

44   **CENTRAL PARK** NAOMI SACHS

46   **CHANGING COURSE** ELIZABETH MOSSOP

48   **CHATTANOOGA** KRISTEN RICHARDS

50   **CHRISTIE WALK** KIRSTY KELLY

52   **THE CITY** THOMAS BALSLEY

54   **CITY REPAIR** JEFF STEIN

56   **COALITIONS** HENK OVINK

58   **COMPANY** BJARKE INGELS

60   **COPENHAGEN'S HARBOR** HELLE LIS SØHOLT

62   **DENSIFICATION** MARK A. FOCHT

64   **DUCHA HALO** JIA YOU

66   **ECO-LODGES** AZIZA CHAOUNI

68 **EL PORVENIR SOCIAL KINDERGARTEN** BARRY BERGDOLL

70 **EMSCHER PARK** ALAN M. BERGER

72 **ENDING ALARM FATIGUE** HUGH LIVINGSTON

74 **ESTUAIRE** MARC ARMENGAUD

76 **FREIBURG** MARCUS VEERMAN

78 **FRUITVALE VILLAGE** LISA RICE

80 **GENERAL MILLS SCULPTURE GARDEN** KONGJIAN YU

82 **GRAND PARIS** NICOLAUS BUCHOUD

84 **GREEN CITY, CLEAN WATERS** INGA SAFFRON

86 **GREEN INFRASTRUCTURE** DIANA BALMORI

88 **GUADALUPE RIVER PARK** WES MICHAELS

90 **THE HIGH LINE** JEFF SHUMAKER

92 **HOLDING PATTERN** JOHN PETERSON

94 **ILLUMINATE** LENI SCHWENDINGER

96 **INHOTIM** TATIANA BILBAO

98 **KHOO TECK PUAT HOSPITAL** TIMOTHY BEATLEY

100 **THE LEICHTAG FOUNDATION RANCH** MIA LEHRER

102 **THE LIGHTNING FIELD** J. MEEJIN YOON

104 **LION'S PARK PLAYSCAPE** MIKYOUNG KIM

106 **LOCAL CODE / REAL ESTATES** KELLER EASTERLING

108 **LONDON CONGESTION PRICING** ANJALI MAHENDRA

110 **MAISON DUFORT** NATHALIE JOLIVERT

112 **MALMÖ** BERT GREGORY

114 **MANY SMALL-SCALE PROJECTS** NINA-MARIE LISTER

116 **MEDIA TIC** DAVID GARCIA

118 **MERIAN MAP OF PARIS** EVA FRANCH I GILABERT

120 **METRO LIBRARIES** ANA LUCIA GONZÁLEZ IBÁÑEZ

122 **THE MIDTOWN GREENWAY** PETER HARNIK

124 **MUSHROOM BOARD** JONSARA RUTH

126 **NEWPORT BEACH CIVIC CENTER AND PARK** JOHN KING

128 **NOS QUEDAMOS** DAMON RICH

130 **OUR KAKA'AKO** JESS ZIMBABWE

132 **PARK(ING) DAY** JANET ECHELMAN

134 **PEDESTRIAN ZONES** KIM YAO

136 **PRIMARY SCHOOL IN GANDO** ANDRES LEPIK

138 **PROJECT ROW HOUSES** F. KAID BENFIELD

140 **REBUILDING CENTER** SARAH MINEKO ICHIOKA

142 **RIVERWALK** MARION WEISS

144 **ROME** JACK SULLIVAN

146 **SAN FRANCISCO BAY** SONJA HINRICHSEN

148 **THE SAND ENGINE** KRISTINA HILL

150 **SCHIEBLOCK** TRACY METZ

152 **SERENBE** MARINA KHOURY

154 **SEVEN DIALS** VICTOR DOVER

156 **SHERBOURNE COMMONS** CHRISTOPHER HUME

158 **SIMS MUNICIPAL RECYCLING FACILITY** ROBERT M. ROGERS

160 **SOLAR ROADWAYS** CHRISTOPH GIELEN

162 **STELLAR APARTMENTS** KATRIN KLINGENBERG

164 **TENNESSEE VALLEY AUTHORITY** DAVID LEVEN

166 **TERMITE MOUNDS** JANINE BENYUS

168 **UNITÉ D'HABITATION** ANTHONY FLINT

170 **VERNACULAR ARCHITECTURE** LI XIAODONG

172 **WIND MEGA COMPLEXES** LESTER BROWN

175 IMAGE CREDITS

176 ACKNOWLEDGMENTS

WE CAN'T GIVE UP YET.

We can't give in to fatalism, or even pessimism, just yet. While we face incredible challenges—with climate change, biodiversity loss, and rising economic inequality at the top of the list—there are glimpses of a more positive, sustainable future here today. In this book, you'll find buildings, landscapes, plans, and works of art—contemporary and historic, but all real—that point the way forward.

I asked each contributor to this book the same question: What gives you hope that a sustainable future is possible? What shows the way forward? If possible, please talk about a project. And please don't talk about anything that you've been involved in.

Contributors were selected in a some-what random fashion. I knew some people and had heard of others, while still others were recommended to me by someone I interviewed. There are architects, landscape architects, urban planners, academics, nonprofit leaders, policymakers, and artists, and some people who cross multiple categories or are beyond these. The contributors come from all over the world, but most are here in the United States. This book represents the collective wisdom of a hive mind, a meeting of so many disciplines. All are deeply committed to creating a more positive future.

Nearly everyone had an answer to the question. Out of more than eighty people I spoke to, only two said, "I don't have much hope for the future." The rest seemed stirred by the challenge. I saw a few people's eyes light up, intrigued by my challenge. Some had answers at the tips of their tongues, as if they had been just been thinking about this. Others asked for time to think, checking their assumptions and beliefs, searching for the right example. While I prompted sometimes, I didn't tell people what others were talking about, so no one was influenced by anyone else.

Almost all contributors were interviewed in person or over the phone. My goal was to keep the tone light and conversational. This is because I fear "design speak." This language, like any other inside jargon, is alienating, elitist, and completely inaccessible to the public. This book is, I hope, part of the antidote to that, too, as it shows a whole range of designers and other professionals who communicate beautifully, in easy to understand terms, with passion. They really connect. So it turns out that my fear was largely unfounded; all the contributors totally got it. That gives me hope for the future because without the ability to communicate with everyone, we have no chance.

Even though all the answers are unique, the ideas and projects share common goals. They fall into loose groups. One group shows that our best hope is in the most cutting-edge technologies: progress toward sustainability means throwing out the old and coming up with new, revolutionary approaches that can undo our broken systems. In contrast, another group shows that what's old—and what has survived and adapted itself to change over many decades—is what's sustainable. The idea is that we don't make them like we used to.

And then other answers tell the story of the social, or community, side of sustainability, expressing the idea that new technologies are all well and good, but if a community doesn't feel a sense of ownership over a project and can't maintain it far into the future, then what good is it? Another side of this is that a sustainable project is one that reinvests in its surrounding community. These projects actively bolster a community's ability to sustain itself.

One set of projects perhaps speak most powerfully to me: these projects teach us—through innovative design and natural beauty—that we are all part of the Earth. They harness nature or mimic its forms.

In doing so, they reconnect us to the land, water, air, quietly letting us know that our ultimate sustainability, our survival, is dependent on a much more complex system. And so many fascinating ideas fall into many of these groups, accomplishing so much at once. Together, they form a much-needed conversation about how to reach a sustainable future.

Some takeaways that leaped out at me (as you read, you may see others):

- We can end our dependence on fossil fuels by shifting to renewable energy. Energy from the sun provides more than we will ever need.

- The world is becoming increasingly urban, and that's not a bad thing. Dense, walkable communities are the most energy-efficient and low-carbon environments we have. But to live in dense communities, people need beautiful streets, parks, waterfronts, and so forth.

- Communities know best what they need and what they can handle. If communities feel empowered, they can solve many of their own problems and plot out their own paths to future sustainability.

- Reinvest in old places, buildings, and traditions; imbue them with new energy.

- Go local for skills and resources. Use what you have, as that will form a language that resonates with the community.

- Use new technologies to reduce energy and water use. Scale up these technologies into broader systems that work at the neighborhood or district level. Make these systems cheaper than the wasteful status quo.

- Invest in people by creating new skills. Who will design and build the most cutting-edge buildings and infrastructure of the future?

- Reuse what you have, waste nothing.

- Create access to nature to improve our health and well-being and teach us to rely on a greater natural system.

- Design with nature. Or, even better, design like nature and mimic the natural forms most efficient at conserving resources.

- Cities sit within metro areas and regions. Go big: consider the metro and regional scale. Sustainability is about creating affordable opportunities in housing, employment, and transportation for regions.

- Bureaucracies, which set policies that affect our health and environment, can evolve and become smarter. Sustainable policies create broader impacts beyond one project.

- Real projects show the way forward. By their very existence, they demonstrate what's possible. Their very success is their reality. And that means they can be replicated, and then become the norm, if we are smart.

And reading through all the answers, I thought again that hope is perhaps the most valuable currency we have, as it motivates all our actions—from creating a world-changing new technology to preserving a beloved old building or town square to protecting a threatened community or ecosystem. We have the answers. We are both the cause of our problems and the solution to them.

As you explore the answers, think about what you would say if someone asked you these questions. Or think about someone you'd like to ask. I bet the answer that you get will be unexpected.

While there is certainly cause for alarm, it's not all bad news. As the science fiction writer William Gibson said, "The future is already here, but it's just not evenly distributed." While he was perhaps thinking of some sort of technodystopia, this could also mean a more sustainable future is on the way. This book offers a glimpse into that more positive future, if we take the time to reconnect with what works today.

THE IDEAS

ABOMEY
SUZANNE PRESTON BLIER

Plan for obsolescence, not just expansion.

Abomey is the capital of the historical West African Kingdom of Dahomey (Republic of Benin). This central plan, walled city was created in the reign of King Agaja (1718–1740 CE). The main palace is in the center, with later palaces, temples, and administrative structures built in a spiral radiating out from the center. This spiral was in essence preplanned, as early planners expected that each successive ruler would take over new land as the city expanded. Planned destruction was key to this process. Today, architects and planners rarely think creatively of obsolescence as part of the design process.

The value placed on earthen architecture in Dahomey is also important. This material is wonderfully malleable—not only in terms of its technical and design features but also in how it enables social change. Sections of earthen buildings are easily removed and rebuilt as family and other needs change. In Dahomey, when the senior man in a family dies, the compound may be abandoned. While this now-abandoned site looks ragged and raw, it is in essence fermenting, and, at some point, maybe two generations later, the family will come together and someone else will rebuild here. The structure and family are in a sense reborn.

Dahomey shows the imperative of strategic planning for obsolescence and the use of materials that can readily be rebuilt. Today in cities we too often push those least able to fight back out of their neighborhoods so new structures can be erected. If one planned for obsolescence as a key part of the design process, much would be gained. Using more malleable materials would enable us to adapt our cities more easily. Shrinkage or growth could be made more consistent with individual and community needs.

Suzanne Preston Blier is an art historian who serves as the Allen Whitehill Clowes Professor of Fine Arts and professor of African and African American studies at Harvard University.

↗

Plan of Abomey, Capital of the Dahomey Kingdom (Republic of Benin), Africa, 1718–1740 CE

15

ACEQUIAS
MAKANI THEMBA

Manage water so future generations have enough of it.

———

Acequias in New Mexico are a five-hundred-year-old water system. They are basically a system for organizing underground water. In New Mexico, water is critical. Acequias are present in so many traditions. They combine engineering, architecture, and human ingenuity.

Spain was heavily influenced by the architectural and engineering traditions of the Moors in North Africa. Spain largely organized its systems around Moorish ones. In turn, Spain brought this system of water management to New Mexico, when the latter was part of Mexico.

The system is part of a neighborhood. There are heads of the waterways, and their responsibilities are passed down from generation to generation. They are guardians of the water and make sure that the water is being accessed properly and used as a shared commodity for this generation and the ones to come.

Newer technology has seeped in. The guardians are using technology to help manage the water supply and follow the latest weather systems. But human knowledge of the water system has been passed down for five hundred years. Today, the managers of the acequias have an association so people can get together and share knowledge.

Acequias bring together the best of technology and design, so humans can lead their best lives. That's really the point of technology and design. Through acequias, we can see the evolution of technology, design, and human beings, and our relationship to each other. Acequias connect us to nature and ourselves.

Makani Themba is executive director of the Praxis Project.

→
Acequia, New Mexico

ANGKOR WAT
RICK COOK

Connect architecture to the natural world.

———

I'm inspired by Angkor Wat in Cambodia. Angkor Wat is beautiful because its architecture is deeply connected with the natural world. Even in its ruined state, Angkor Wat is an optimistic place.

This temple complex, which was built in the twelfth century, is the largest on Earth. In the preindustrial era, Angkor City was actually the world's most populated city.

The temple complex is supported by a hydraulic engine—eastern and western pools, which are called barays. They are entirely handmade. While the eastern baray is now dry, the western one still holds acres of water. The western baray is larger than Central Park in New York City.

Khmer culture prospered between the tenth and fifteenth centuries because the Khmer were wise stewards of a precious natural resource: water. Khmer culture is a monsoon one. Even its calendar is arranged around the cycle of wet and dry periods. Angkor Wat's pools, which were imbued with a spiritual quality, were built so that an extra crop could be grown in the dry season.

But some experts believe that the pools were also built because of Cambodia's extremely hot climate. The pools function as evaporative cooling towers or plate heat exchanges, creating cooling breezes. Buildings are oriented to block out the harshest sun, and deep-shaded walkways provide access to the stone temples, which are hollow with a narrow aperture at the top. Breezes then move across the pools down the pathways into the holy centers of temples, which are thermal chimneys. Essentially, the Khmer created air conditioning.

We are just beginning to understand the complex geometry and proportions of Angkor Wat.

Rick Cook is founder and principal of Cook + Fox.

→

Angkor Wat, Siem Reap, Cambodia

ANN DEMEULEMEESTER SHOP
MARC KUSHNER

Let the landscape encroach on buildings.

———

The public loves green walls, walls that are literally green. Architects often raise their eyebrows at this trend, as we tend to think that they are a bit hackneyed and just the latest form of greenwashing. But I think that we should celebrate green walls, as they show that people want a closer connection to the natural environment, that they are fed up with the strict dichotomy between the built and the natural. People want a merging of the two.

One great example of this, the Ann Demeulemeester Shop, is in Seoul, South Korea, designed by Minsuk Cho.

It's easy to dismiss this amazing building as "trendy" or green-washed and not truly ecologically relevant. But the public loves buildings like this. People get really excited.

If you play out this populist trend, we could have less need for air conditioning and more access to daylight, better ventilation, and improved energy conservation. This trend may then foretell a more sustainable way to occupy built spaces.

If the public desires something other than a concrete box set in a landscape, the green wall also gives architects license to bring the natural world into the built world in a substantial—not just decorative—way. It's not us versus nature. Maybe there is a new way, a new rule set. The landscape can encroach on buildings. We should embrace that.

Marc Kushner is a partner at the architectural firm Hollwich Kushner and CEO of Architizer.com.

→
Ann Demeulemeester Shop, Seoul, South Korea

LAS ARBOLEDAS
MARIA BELLALTA

Make sustainability art we can relate to.

The architect Luis Barragán's landscape Las Arboledas has all the raw elements of sustainability.

In 1962 near Mexico City, Barragán created this simple place. Soil on the ground was compacted. Giant eucalyptus trees were planted in a straight line. A long trough made out of concrete was built, called Fuente del Bebedero. Water is collected and then cascades out of the trough, like a pool with no edges. In the background, at one end of the trough, there's a white concrete wall juxtaposed with the horizontal plane. Shadows of the trees are projected onto the wall.

It was created for horses to drink from, but today kids from the area come to splash around and bathe.

Las Arboledas collects water simply. There are robust trees that provide shade and grow on their own (they are not irrigated).

Nothing at Las Arboledas is artificial. It's a reminder of what we need to go back to. It shows us how we can get down to the elements and just keep what we need.

It's an encounter with the essential that provokes a way to think about what we need to do in the future.

Las Arboledas shows us the artistic, cultural side to sustainability. It's not a contraption that you can't relate to. We need to get back to this level of art. Sustainability can be art, mechanically and spatially.

Maria Bellalta is head of the School of Landscape Architecture at Boston Architectural College.

→
Las Arboledas, Mexico City

ARTISTS FOR HUMANITY
JASON SCHUPBACH

Expand sustainability past the building, into the community.

———

Artists for Humanity has tendrils extending throughout Boston. In 2004 it created its green headquarters, called the EpiCenter, which was the first LEED-platinum building in postindustrial South Boston. There, the group is teaching middle school students from tough communities how to be productive and showing them how to get real jobs in the arts and design.

The group is bursting at the seams and so is planning a major green expansion. At the new center, Artists for Humanity will be teaching seven hundred kids.

Artists for Humanity will act as an incubator, creating "maker spaces" for innovative new green products and companies. The group is about recycling everything. The current center has cool features like banisters made from used car windshields.

Anyone can commission the group to create something. It is famous for making great tables out of magazines, and the mayor's office just commissioned it to create all office tables. And it has sold millions in student artwork and design services.

Artists for Humanity is not just about building green, but about social sustainability and creating resiliency in our communities. Sustainability can't be limited just to the building.

Jason Schupbach is director of design programs for the National Endowment for the Arts, where he oversees all design and creative placemaking, grants, and partnerships.

→
The EpiCenter, Boston

BEDZED
JEMMA GREEN

Every country: Create a living laboratory for sustainable housing.

———

The Beddington Zero Energy Development (BedZED) is a carbon-emission-free housing and office development in Hackbridge, London.

Constructed between 2000 and 2002, BedZED was the first project of its kind to think not only about the embodied energy of the building materials and the operational energy from the residents in the buildings, but also about the environmental impacts of the residents and users outside the building, such as transportation to and from work and air travel.

Although the project is more than a decade old, BedZED is still a beacon of inspiration. BedZED uses 100 percent renewable energy, something very few developments around the world have managed to do since. BedZED endures as a leader in sustainable design. It has triggered more sustainable urban planning in the United Kingdom. The project has taught us the things that didn't work so well, such as the black water–recycling scheme, but also the many things that did work well.

In a place like Australia or other hotter climates where there is abundant sunshine, one might think that solar panels on houses are the norm. And while the use of rooftop solar panels is growing very fast, buildings are not ordinarily designed to optimize for the use of solar energy. Developers are cautious about spending too much on environmental initiatives for fear of not getting a return on their investment.

Every country needs a living laboratory such as BedZED to start a bigger conversation about what's possible in sustainable housing. Although BedZED is unique to the British climate and lifestyle, we can look to projects like this to orient our buildings with the seasons and our finite resources.

Jemma Green is a research fellow and doctoral candidate at Curtin University Sustainability Policy Institute in Fremantle, Australia.

→
Beddington Zero Energy Development (BedZED), London

BEFORE I DIE
PAUL FARMER

Engage people on their own terms.

———

Candy Chang is a planner, journalist, and artist. She became famous for her *Before I Die* project, which has been replicated in so many places, the way a building or landscape never is. In this project, Chang turned a wall into a blackboard and left chalk so people could write their own hopes anonymously.

Planning is about stories, and planners must be great storytellers. Planning is a conversation, not a monologue or even a dialogue. Chang has taken all this and come up with an artwork of civic engagement. She operates at the intersection of art and planning. Her work is one of the most remarkable examples of this that I've ever seen.

I've sat through more nighttime public meetings than I can remember. Attending those, I've found it's hard to reach people beyond the usual ones who show up. Before social media, I called them the people who don't watch TV. Planners also reach people through rotary clubs and interfaith groups. They use many ways to engage people. Chang has added richness to the options.

But another problem is that planners often set goals and objectives and try to get everyone to agree to those. But no one wakes up in the morning and says I need to set a goal and then checks in at the end of the night to see if he or she has achieved measurable objectives. No one operates this way.

We want to engage people about their hopes, desires, and fears. But it has to be on their own terms, not those of the planners and architects.

If you ask people what you like or don't like, you can get to their gut feelings, which leads to honesty. They then speak in a way that's not foreign to them. Everyone knows what they like and dislike, where they are trying to go, what their hopes are for themselves and their neighborhood.

Chang's first wall in New Orleans conveys all those hopes. It's a technique for making very private thoughts public and creating a conversation about them. If you had a public meeting, people would be very guarded. A blackboard and chalk are simple but achieve a lot.

Paul Farmer is CEO of the American Planning Association.

→

Before I Die, New Orleans

CHANGE THE WORLD

Do it all

FALL IN LOVE

MEET ELLE

JUST

FEEL

OPEN MYSELF UP

Before I die I want to _____ him to love me.

Before I die I want to _____ GET A TATTOO   LIVE/America

Before I die I want to _____ Change the World!!!

Before I die I want to _____ LEGALIZE HERB

Before I die I want to _____ repeat the 3-peat! Live in

Before I die I want to _____ Sing/Dance

Before I die I want to _____

Before I die I want to
Before I die I want to
Before I die I want to
Before I die I want to   MAKE MY
Before I die I want to   PROUD
Before I die I want to

See the world ♥ AECM   Leave the world a better place   ghost

SAVE A ♥ Before

Rockstar   LIFE   Reach Nirvana

I want to be all I   (happy)

meone truly Happy

WANT TO B A CEO
be a doctor
and save
lives

eBRON James

Discover w/my bro   Lily T   Travel the World   Dive the Gre Barrier

BIOMIMICRY AND BIODESIGN
BLAINE BROWNELL

Partner with building materials instead of killing them.

———

Biomimicry and biodesign—which involve creating lifelike or living systems, products, and technologies—give me hope about the future.

Several architects and engineers are using algae—living, photosynthesizing microbes—in building facades. The engineering firm Arup created a promising system for a German building expo: It has a living algae curtain wall, which harvests the building's algae as an energy source through a bioreactor.

Algae are pumped through the system and harvested for biomass, and then new algae are circulated in. As the algae circulate through the facade, they provide solar shading and thermal insulation. The advantage of the system is that it takes what is typically an eyesore in nature and makes use of its photosynthetic capabilities.

Why algae? Why use in a high-tech wall? That's the intriguing part. This system is about synthesizing industrial technology with living organisms. It's about harvesting nature in a new way. In the industrial way, we mine and then process materials, essentially killing them. This is how we work with trees and other plant fibers. Now, we can allow natural materials to play out their natural lives. We can harvest materials on-site in a form of agricultural architecture instead of using the old energy plant.

Blaine Brownell is associate professor at the University of Minnesota School of Architecture and author of Material Strategies: Innovative Applications in Architecture.

→
Solar Leaf Project, International Building Exhibition, Hamburg, Germany, 2013

BRADDOCK, PENNSYLVANIA
THOMAS WOLTZ

Don't erase the construct of the past; be creative about how to adapt it.

———

Braddock, Pennsylvania, is a historical community reenvisioning its abandoned, formerly toxic lands with urban farming and community initiatives. Braddock has so much potential energy. It's about to become something, a place where people want to move.

In the 1870s Andrew Carnegie created the first steel mill using the Bessemer process in Braddock, and he created his first public library for the workers. That library later became the model for the Carnegie Library system. Carnegie was interested in the well-being of the workers from a physical and cultural perspective. Now, the library functions as a center of community life, and you can take tours of it.

Hope can be a catalyst for the community. In Braddock today, the community is pooling resources, building an urban farm, starting youth programs, and attracting artists. Braddock is reusing its old infrastructure: the roads, sewers, and rail. It is adaptively reusing industrial infrastructure. This place has so much embodied history and culture. By reinvigorating those things, the community won't be lost.

The Grow Pittsburgh organization built a farm, Braddock Youth Project offers mentoring and classes, and Mayor John Fetterman led Braddock Redux, a community revitalization effort. He is an amazing guy: six foot eight, with a master's in public administration from Harvard University. He moved to Braddock in 2001 and is a real testament to how a few people with vision can turn depressed places around.

It takes hard work to create a place, and it takes a long time. As a counterpoint to greenfield development, Braddock is working with what it has, adding to the existing meaning, starting a new layer. It is building into the bones already there.

There are so many postindustrial places with great value. It's important not to erase the construct of the past but to be creative about how we adapt it. My hope is that we value, preserve, and honor old constructs while finding creative reuses.

Infrastructure projects of the last century are often found on the edges of society, the periphery. It's important to bring these edges into people's daily reality. The rejuvenation of derelict places can sometimes create a new sense of community.

Thomas Woltz is principal and owner of Nelson Byrd Woltz Landscape Architects, and in 2013 was recognized as design innovator of the year by the Wall Street Journal Magazine.

→

Braddock, Pennsylvania

THE BRITISH AMBASSADOR'S RESIDENCE
LEO A. DALY III

Invest in older buildings, rather than tear them down.

———

The British Ambassador's residence in Washington, D.C., was designed by Sir Edwin Lutyens, one of the greatest British architects, whose ideas were very advanced for the late 1920s.

The design of the residence is fantastic. It's classical in style and influenced by colonial American and traditional English architecture. The details are extraordinary— the depth of the windowsills; the space above the doors; the setback of the French doors; the stone and ironwork. We could not build this level of quality construction today.

Lutyens used his knowledge of sun path, airflow, shading, ceiling height, and wall thickness to save money on energy. The walls of the house are exceptionally thick, varying between sixteen and twenty-six inches (41–66 cm). Some are brick and stone veneer; others are solid brick. We don't build walls like this anymore; they require too much manpower and are too expensive.

Lutyens also designed extensive gardens with trees and shrubs to shade and protect the house. Over the years these gardens have been enhanced to provide further privacy, security, and noise reduction. They benefit the environment, too.

It is important to note the value of the energy expended on building a property like this. It is called "embodied energy." According to the Environmental Protection Agency, for a new sustainable building, using 40 percent recycled materials, it will take sixty-five years to make up for the emissions produced from demolishing a comparable existing building.

So, it is often more environmentally efficient to preserve these old buildings, rather than tear them down and replace them with a new LEED-certified one.

The British Ambassador's residence has been updated many times during its eighty-year-plus history. It has survived the tenure of twenty-two ambassadors, their families, and staff.

Recent upgrades include energy-efficient lighting throughout, with solar panels gracing the outbuildings. There is a new energy-efficient roof on the adjacent chancery building and a new energy-efficient power generator. A new rainwater-harvesting system on the roof is used to water the extensive gardens.

I think it is a shame that we don't invest more often in old buildings. I certainly believe in preserving a special building like this!

Leo A. Daly III is chairman and CEO of Leo A. Daly Associates.

↗
British Ambassador's Residence, Washington, D.C.

BUCKMINSTER FULLER'S DYMAXION MAP
MARIA AIOLOVA

Create a continuous flow of energy between all continents.

———

Buckminster Fuller's Dymaxion Map is a projection that unfolded the world to reveal that all the continents are interconnected. This map, created in 1943, shows that it is conceivable to create a continuous flow of energy and resources between all continents.

Projecting into the future, the map can be used to envision a global energy grid supplying new energy from the sun during the day and thermal sources at night. Energy can then be moved to wherever it's most needed in the world.

Fuller's thinking still applies today. The ideas have not changed, but the technology is now available. We can connect every energy source around the world. Offshore wind turbines in the North Sea could be linked to photovoltaic arrays in sub-Saharan Africa. Together, these two energy sources could power all of Europe.

The Dymaxion Map shows us a global way of thinking, a new way of conceiving the world. Through the theories developed by Buckminster Fuller, we can redirect energy resources to high population areas, the place where energy is most needed. We can also reach all those places urban planners have forgotten.

Maria Aiolova is cofounder of Terreform ONE and academic director for Global Architecture and Design at CIEE.

→
The Fuller Projection Map design is a trademark of the Buckminster Fuller Institute

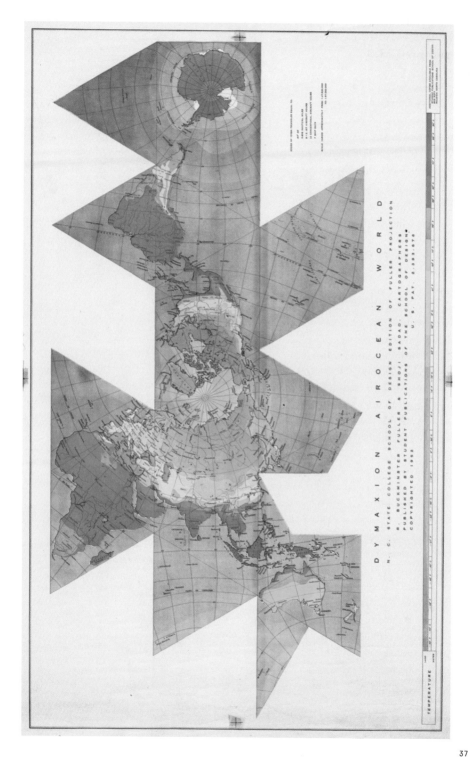

DYMAXION AIROCEAN WORLD

N. C. STATE COLLEGE SCHOOL OF DESIGN EDITION OF FULLER PROJECTION

R. BUCKMINSTER FULLER & SHOJI SADAO, CARTOGRAPHERS
PUBLISHED BY STUDENT PUBLICATIONS OF THE SCHOOL OF DESIGN
COPYRIGHTED 1952   U. S. PAT. 2,393,676

THE BURNHAM PLAN
TERESA CÓRDOVA

Use master plans to rebuild neighborhoods—not destroy them.

———

Chicago is still benefiting from the Burnham Plan, the name commonly used for the 1909 Plan of Chicago. The architects and planners Daniel Burnham and Edward H. Bennett created the plan in collaboration with the Commercial Club of Chicago.

One thing I like most about the plan is that Burnham and Bennett established the lakefront as public space. Even today, that's one of the unique features of Chicago. Other cities privatize their waterfronts. Chicago has more public waterfront than any other major U.S. city.

Along the lakefront and throughout the city, Burnham and Bennett created great parks. Today they are used for festivals, concerts, games, and gatherings. People walk or bike through them, enjoying the land and waterfront.

The plan also created a set of civic and cultural centers, such as the Field Museum and Adler Planetarium. So many great public cultural amenities came out of the plan.

Burnham and Bennett also laid out the first regional transportation system linking southern Wisconsin and northwestern Indiana. They thought about how people would get into the city and how they would move around the city. There was also a comprehensive strategy for moving freight in and out of the city, so that Chicago would remain a hub for the transportation of goods.

The plan came out of the City Beautiful movement and is considered its high point. The plan was informed by the idea that a commercially efficient city could also be aesthetically pleasing, and so the city was filled with beautiful architecture and public spaces.

The plan was the first comprehensive attempt to reshape a major American city and create a culture of planning. Although the plan was popular, it had some shortcomings: it never addressed social issues, such as housing and the condition of the city's working poor. Chicago is only as great as its neighborhoods. The plan can inspire us to rebuild them. We must use the principles of the master plan to make places functional and beautiful and to meet economic and social needs. Master planning needs to be about rebuilding neighborhoods—not destroying them.

We need to see the larger vision of what's possible, as embodied in the 1909 Plan of Chicago. We need holistic planning that starts with a connection to nature.

Teresa Córdova is director of the University of Illinois at Chicago's Great Cities Institute and is professor of urban planning and policy in the College of Urban Planning and Public Affairs.

↗
Plan of Chicago, by Daniel Burnham, 1909

BUTARO HOSPITAL
JOHN CARY

Improve health by providing access to nature.

My wife and I gave birth to a beautiful baby girl in November 2013. We went to a world-class hospital in Berkeley, California, yet the room we spent three full days in had no natural light, just bright, glaring lights that didn't even have dimmers. On the wall facing my wife was a clock, as if expectant mothers would ever want to watch the seconds tick by.

While there, we thought of the Butaro Hospital in rural Rwanda, which we had visited earlier in the year. The project was designed by MASS Design Group for Partners in Health and the Rwandan Ministry of Health. It is the last of ten district hospitals to be built in Rwanda, bringing care to a community of 340,000 people. And it is one of the most beautiful and dignified places I have ever been. As Dr. Paul Farmer, founder of Partners in Health, said, "If you can build this here, you can build anything anywhere." The hospital didn't even have electricity right before it opened.

The Butaro Hospital was designed contrary to most architectural and design practices followed in the United States. Instead of a central corridor—which is often a conduit for spreading communicable diseases—the corridor is put on the exterior of the building. It's covered, which works with the climate. Every single bed faces a window. Looking straight through their toes ten to fifteen feet ahead, patients have breathtaking views of nature. Research shows that access to nature and natural light have beneficial health outcomes.

There are many other positive, sustainable outcomes as well. The hospital was built with all local labor using local materials. Local workers dug the foundation by hand, which meant that they didn't have to bring in an excavator from Kigali, four hours away. Some four thousand people were employed, creating new skills they can market. Women masons who worked on the project are some of the most sought-after in Rwanda now. As a result, the Butaro Hospital was built at half the cost and in two-thirds the time of other district hospitals.

This is one of the most sustainable projects I can point to, but not in the standard LEED understanding of the word; the Butaro Hospital was designed to improve health by providing access to nature, and that's exactly what it has done.

John Cary is a curator and strategist for TED, founder of PublicInterestDesign.org, founding curator of the Autodesk Foundation, and author of The Power of Pro Bono.

↗
Butaro Hospital, Rwanda

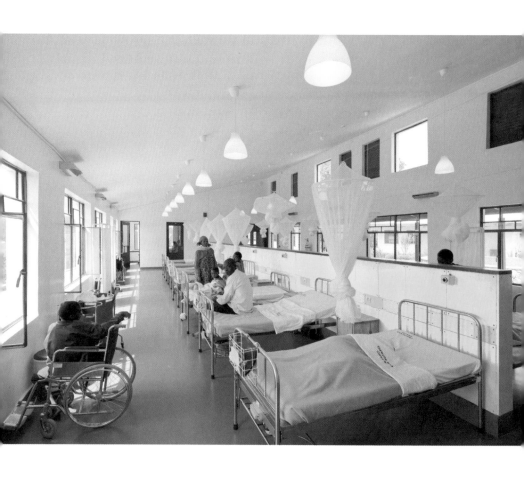

CALW
CHRISTIAN GABRIEL

Overlap land uses, enjoy the curious wrinkles.

———

My family is from Calw, a small historical city in Germany. It's in the Black Forest region, near the border with Switzerland. It's where the author Herman Hesse is from. This quintessential minor urban city is set within a majestic environment. There's a meshed relationship between the city and the surrounding nature. The fully functional town center, with its park system, well-preserved waterway, architectural character, and dense, highly connected streets, is deeply linked with the environment.

The locals are stewards of Calw's forests, natural springs, and agricultural land. There is a reciprocal relationship between the town and everything around it. But there is also visionary architecture: this is not a place trapped in the past.

Everyone points to Germany as an example of progressive development. Germany did this or that supergreen development, using integrated design. But these new green projects are often created from the developers' standpoint. There is a singularity to the land use. These new projects may realize the highest levels of sustainable performance, but they are still separate—they just mimic the traditional approach.

Calw's historic city center has overlapping land uses. The curious wrinkles are what make it so appealing. It is multilayered in the same way that New York City is. It's layered and diverse, providing a model for postindustrial minor cities. Calw provides us all with a precedent for how to move minor cities forward in a new direction.

Calw has a certain efficiency that's aspirational. There's a productive landscape that people want to preserve. The forests are really used; there is intensive arboriculture, which makes them as constructed a landscape as Central Park in New York City. There's a rich pluralism.

Christian Gabriel is national design director of landscape architecture for the Office of the Chief Architect at the U.S. General Services Administration.

→
Calw, Germany

CENTRAL PARK
NAOMI SACHS

Create the presence of nearby nature.

———

Frederick Law Olmsted got it, and so much earlier than others: He knew nature is essential to our health and well-being. Before he became a landscape architect, he was executive secretary for the U.S. Sanitation Commission (now the Red Cross). With Calvert Vaux, he created Central Park in New York City to connect people with nature.

In the late 1800s infectious diseases like influenza and tuberculosis were the leading causes of death in the United States. Overcrowding and poor sanitation were partly to blame. In many cities people were so desperate for nature that they picnicked in cemeteries, the only parklike settings at the time. Olmsted knew this and realized that people needed parks.

Central Park is not only "the lungs of the city"—it's the largest green space in Manhattan—but it's also one of the most democratic, just as Olmsted intended. People of all ages, races, and classes can gather there on an equal basis, without having to pay, except perhaps to buy an ice cream. There are all types of programs going on, like Shakespeare in the Park, art installations like The Gates by Christo and Jeanne-Claude, concerts, marches, and demonstrations.

Beauty and aesthetics were important to Olmsted. People think that the park came with all those trees and rocks, but Olmsted put those trees in, moved rocks from here to there, built the ponds and lakes. It was designed to make you feel as if you are in a pastoral landscape that has always been there.

Central Park has existed for 160 years, and it hasn't changed much. The fact that it's been here so long and is beloved by so many people means that it will likely continue far into the future. It's not a new project that may or may not be successful; it has stood the test of time. That is an important part of sustainability. It's also an incredible habitat for all flora and fauna, including people.

More and more research is correlating the presence of "nearby nature" with people's positive health and well-being. Central Park is one of the best and most inspiring examples of nearby nature in the world.

Naomi Sachs is founding director of the Therapeutic Landscapes Network and coauthor of Therapeutic Landscapes: An Evidence-Based Approach to Designing Healing Gardens and Restorative Landscapes.

→

Central Park, New York

CHANGING COURSE
ELIZABETH MOSSOP

Use creativity to influence established systems.

———

What makes me particularly optimistic about the future is the Changing Course competition, organized by the Environmental Defense Fund and Van Alen Institute. Who would have thought ten years ago that there could be a major rethinking of the way in which the Mississippi River is managed?

A broad coalition of interests is coming together to move the public discourse: Privately funded nonprofit organizations are cooperating with the state, the U.S. Army Corps of Engineers, international consulting firms, and academic institutions to generate ideas and develop a new paradigm for the river.

While there is no guarantee that any of the winning concepts will be implemented, the competition is a test to see if there is a way for creativity to influence a river and land management system that has consistently produced bad outcomes for the public, as evidenced by the incredible loss of wetlands along the river and the huge amount of pollution that enters the Gulf of Mexico. These outcomes are a result of designing to solve a single issue as opposed to taking into consideration all the cultural and ecological factors that make a complex system operate.

The transitional posthurricane environment in Louisiana is producing interesting and unexpected outcomes that would not have been possible before Katrina. This is a moment of rich opportunity for designers to assert themselves in processes that are traditionally dominated by engineers and scientists. We must seize these key opportunities as we change the culture around issues of big infrastructure and land management.

Elizabeth Mossop is a founding principal of Spackman Mossop + Michaels and professor of landscape architecture at Louisiana State University.

↗

Marsh in Pass-a-Loutre Wildlife Management Area, Plaquemines Parish, Louisiana

CHATTANOOGA
KRISTEN RICHARDS

Humanize and populate the urban core in responsible, sustainable ways.

I began visiting Chattanooga, Tennessee, about thirty years ago to see relatives who live on nearby Signal Mountain. There were few reasons to go downtown other than the Chattanooga Choo Choo and a few fun, funky bars and pool halls. The wonderful Hunter Museum of American Art sits on a beautiful bluff above the Tennessee River that, back then, didn't have a whole lot of "beautiful" to look over. The river was polluted, and both shores were lined with long-abandoned industrial brownfield properties, and our car doors stayed locked at all times when driving—until our return to bucolic Signal Mountain.

Fast forward three decades. The Choo Choo is now accessible via free electric buses that connect the station to the riverfront— reclaimed as the delightful, eight-mile-long Chattanooga Riverwalk. In between are two outstanding aquariums, the Creative Discovery Museum, shops and eateries in restored nineteenth-century buildings (many with housing or offices above), and new, thoughtfully designed, mixed-use apartment complexes with lively, street-level businesses.

The 1891 Walnut Street Bridge was closed to vehicular traffic in 1978 and was scheduled for demolition until planners and community activists stepped in. It reopened in 1993 as a pedestrian (and now dog-friendly!) bridge linking Chattanooga's downtown with the Northshore District on the opposite bank of the river. That district is now brimming with waterfront parks and attractions and a burgeoning community.

None of this happened quickly or easily. There were political, economic, and social hurdles to jump, and it took time, patience, fortitude, and vision. Chattanooga was the groundbreaking model that other cities started paying attention to. It offers important lessons in what to do—and what not to do—to humanize and populate an urban core in responsible, sustainable ways. Now that cities like Houston and Detroit are held up as current models, you know that times are changing. It's taking longer than most of us would like, but change is happening. So cheers to the communities, politicians, Yes-in-My-Backyard (YIMBY) people, and even Not-in-My-Backyard (NIMBY) people, for giving us hope—and carrying on!

Kristen Richards is cofounder and editor of ArchNewsNow.com, and editor in chief of the AIA New York chapter's quarterly journal, Oculus.

→
Chattanooga Riverwalk, Tennessee

CHRISTIE WALK
KIRSTY KELLY

Show people multifamily housing is sustainable.

———

The project I find inspiring is called Christie Walk in Adelaide, Australia, my hometown. It's a sustainable urban village in the heart of the central city, created by a nonprofit group called Urban Ecology Australia and finished in 2006.

Christie Walk was built with sustainability principles, but at its core, it's about community. It pays attention to energy and waste, those kinds of environmental elements, but it also offers affordable housing. It has created a sense of community for different age groups and types of people.

Christie Walk demonstrates that multifamily housing is sustainable, but also very livable. There are townhouses and apartments about five stories in height. But it's still human-scale.

It's very green. There is vegetation everywhere, including on the roofs, and there's a frog pond.

The nonprofit that started it collected a group of like-minded people who wanted to make this concept work in a high-density environment, not just some isolated community out in the woods.

The project's ethos is that if you want sustainable outcomes, people need to support them. It was collectively designed, with a lot of learning by everyone along the way.

Everyone who lives there also teaches others. They occasionally have open houses, when they show people from around Adelaide how they live.

There's a real warmth to the place. It's a great little spot.

Kirsty Kelly is CEO of the Planning Institute of Australia.

→

Christie Walk, Adelaide, Australia

THE CITY
THOMAS BALSLEY

Save our environment with the city.

This invention called the *city* gives me
hope for the future of the planet. People
have discovered how to live together
in a collaborative, cooperative, communal
manner. The urbanization of the entire
world gives me hope.

Moving into cities is the best we can
do to save our environment. Some people
may scoff and say that cities have destroyed
our environment, but imagine what it
would look like if all seven billion of us lived
without cities. Imagine the impact on the
environment if that happened. There would
be no environment to save.

This invention called the *city* impresses
me. It's a phenomenal device. Great thinkers
since the Greeks and earlier have seen
why the city works and what it means for
humanity. It's key to the preservation
of the planet. I'm putting all my money
on the city.

*Thomas Balsley is founder and
principal at Thomas Balsley Associates
in New York.*

→
Tokyo Tower, Japan

CITY REPAIR
JEFF STEIN

**Create a really beautiful place, and
people will slow down to be a part of it.**

———

"Grow where you're planted" is a famous
saying of the traditional Hopi people.
It's what the placemaker Mark Lakeman
has done, who has spent most of his life in
Portland, Oregon, where in 1996 he began
growing the City Repair Project.

Through City Repair, communities of
volunteers have built over three hundred
sustainable works in Portland, making places
that connect people to each other and their
city. City Repair shows a way to reclaim
and repopulate public space to help make
cities sustainable in the long run.

Lakeman's placemaking is a result of
good parenting. I smile when I say that, but
it's true: his father, the architect Michael
Lakeman, founded the urban design division
of Portland's planning department and
helped create Portland's Pioneer Courthouse
Square. His mother, the architecture
professor Sandra Davis Lakeman, concen-
trated on design and public space and is
famous for her investigations of natural
light and the Italian piazza.

American cities west of the Ohio River
were planned by the Continental Congress's
Land Ordinance of 1785, which organized
most of America into a Roman colonial grid.
As Americans, we have the right to free
assembly, yet our gridded American cities
have fewer public spaces than cities in
any other developed country, so we have
no place to do it: streets and intersections
but no piazzas, plazas, or gathering spaces.
In Portland, or Phoenix near where I live,
the grid extends as far as you can see.
But it's about cars and separation—not
places people can belong to.

City Repair is reclaiming street intersections. Volunteers have painted them over,
planted around them, and even depaved
them, taking up the asphalt and replacing
it with pavers or bricks. Create a really
beautiful place, and people will slow
down to be a part of it. What has followed
at these intersections is bulletin boards,
meeting places, even pop-up teahouses.
Here is character, lovability, and work that
is sustaining a community.

In too many locales if you try to organize
a gathering place, officials will point out,
"That's public space, no one can use that."
It happened at Mark Lakeman's first project.
But three hundred projects later, placemaking
has proved to be at the core of sustainability.

*Jeff Stein is president of Paolo Soleri's urban
research institute, Cosanti Foundation.*

→
City Repair Project, Portland, Oregon

COALITIONS
HENK OVINK

Come together to change the world.

I'm inspired when people bypass their own self-interest and form coalitions to do the right thing. This gives sustainability a chance.

Cities like Amsterdam, New York, and Istanbul developed through the ages and came out of a complex, collaborative process that employed design and innovation.

Amsterdam, a city at the crossroads of global trade, was built from a collective process led by merchants. These traders had found the right place to invest in, so they financed planning, design, and engineering to give Amsterdam a high urban quality, which it still has today. The merchants financed the canal infrastructure at the heart of the city, which is still there. The canal shows that with the right collaboration, there can be sustained cultural, environmental, and economic value over the ages.

(By the way, the same is true of the public spaces in many of Holland's old city centers. A recent economic assessment report found that enormous economic and social value was generated from these cities' historic centers, which were also financed through coalitions. These are places that don't just look good; they feel good.)

In New York City there is constant innovation. The city has done things on the spot, making decisions on the ground that immediately work, add value, and become part of the city. Coalitions in New York City have sped up regulatory processes and used pilot tests to make the exception to the normal rules. There are good and bad sides to this. With faster development, you don't always get the value you want, but you can quickly undo mistakes.

In Istanbul projected plans for a third bridge over the Bosphorus Strait immediately created demand for development in the greater metropolitan region. In Arnavutköy the community learned that this new bridge would negatively affect the complex water basins key to the survival of the city and the greater Istanbul region. A coalition was formed involving these layers of interests—the mayor, universities, water services department, development agencies, and Dutch and Flemish designers—to protect the basins. They saw that their landscape is critical to their economy, and water is critical to their survival.

People can still come together and change the world.

Henk Ovink leads the Rebuild by Design competition and is senior adviser to Shaun Donovan, secretary of the U.S. Department of Housing and Urban Development, and to the Hurricane Sandy Rebuilding Task Force.

↗

Courtyard of the Exchange in Amsterdam, by Emanuel de Witte, Museum Boijmans Van Beuningen, Rotterdam, the Netherlands, 1653

Revitalize industrial traditions with contemporary designs.

———

A Finnish-Korean firm called Company travels to places with a rich industrial heritage—Belgium, Germany, South Korea, Russia, Finland—and works with the local craftspeople to create new products in a contemporary way while demonstrating the skills of the industrial traditions.

Company designs these incredibly charming products. One is called "Car Shoes," made in Busan, South Korea. The shoes look like race cars: one shoe has the race car driver Michael Schumacher and the other has the driver Kimi Raikkonen. As you walk, it looks as if they are racing each other.

Another is called the "Winter Tie," which was created with an old Finnish manufacturer. It's a hybrid between a scarf and a tie.

There's a very nice pair of felt shoes called "Dance Shoes," also from Finland. They are made for a father. On top of his shoe, there's a much smaller shoe made for his daughter, a place for her when they are dancing together.

Company collaborated in South Korea with craftspeople to create "Noodle Shoes," a pair of sneakers whose laces sit on top like noodles, a curly ornament. They are selling quite well. The "Bibimbag," named after the famous spicy Korean dish, "keeps all your ingredients separate."

There's a very nice bag from Bavaria, a region famous for sausages and leather products. Company went into a leather factory and collaborated with the factory workers to create the incredibly feminine and elegant "Metal Bag," which is made out of the chain mail used in butcher's gloves.

Rather than apply a universal approach, these products are about taking the time and care to discover local conditions. Company looks at each situation, culture, and climate in a specific way and tries to evolve or invent an approach that gets the maximum amount of impact out of available resources. It's about creating designs tailored to local cultures.

Bjarke Ingels is founding partner of the architecture and urban design firm BIG.

↗

(clockwise from top left) Metal Bag, Car Shoes, Winter Tie, and Dance Shoes, all products designed by Company

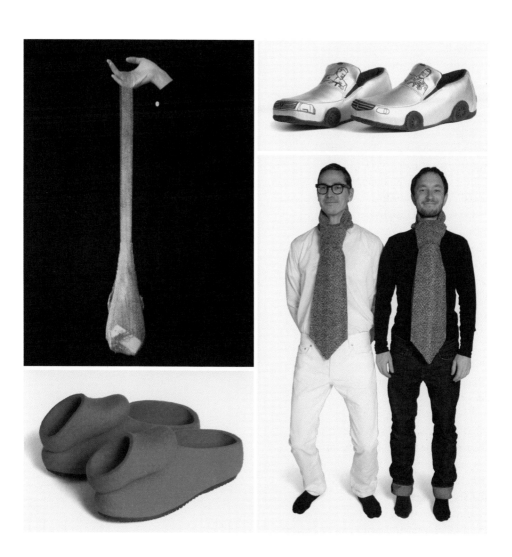

COPENHAGEN'S HARBOR
HELLE LIS SØHOLT

Live with your waterfront; improve your quality of life.

———

Copenhagen was a medieval city that looked inward, but recently it created a new relationship with its harbor. What was once an industrial area, the backside of the city, has become a source of recreation, the frontside.

One thing that helped achieve this was a series of public harbor swimming pools, filled with seawater, created by the Copenhagen city government. One pool was designed by the Danish architect Bjarke Ingels. They are all free of charge, and the city maintains them and provides lifeguards.

These pools are the result of a thirty-to-forty-year process led by the national and city governments. Both governments collaborated on an inner-city clean up program to move polluting industries elsewhere and to create green storm water management systems. The harbor is so clean today that you can jump in and have a swim!

There are also new bicycle bridges that connect Copenhagen to the harbor. One bridge, which is up in the air, is called the Red Cycle Snake. These bridges connect Copenhageners to places previously difficult to reach.

Copenhagen also just turned one stretch of industrial waterfront into a mile-long public park, with its own beach. This part of the city has become one of the most popular to visit and inhabit. You see people kiteboarding, jogging, paddleboating, sunbathing,

or swimming—which they do even in the winter. This park is one of the most democratic spaces in Copenhagen, attracting many different ethnic groups, much more so than our traditional squares. The beach park is not influenced by commercial interests as traditional squares are with their café culture and shopping. The beach park offers a variety of recreational activities attractive to a greater diversity of people throughout the year.

Together, these projects show a new way to move around and live with the harbor. It's a fantastic story, but it took a lot of effort over the decades and a persistent implementation of sustainability.

So many cities were built along waterways—to move goods and people. For too long we've used those waterways as an industrial zone instead of a recreation zone. The story of Copenhagen is about creating a good quality of life for people. Our story can be aspirational for other cities with waterfronts.

Helle Lis Søholt is founding partner and CEO of Gehl Architects.

↗

Copenhagen Harbor beaches, bicycle bridges, and swimming facilities

DENSIFICATION
MARK A. FOCHT

Use urban public spaces to create acceptance of diversity.

———

The continuing densification of cities gives me hope. People are coming back to cities because they understand the intrinsic value of life in cities. Cities are diverse places where people can find common ground. Suburbs and rural areas can be isolating because residents are not forced to live with other people.

As cities become even more vertical, the common ground is shared streets and parks. Public spaces are where different kinds of people interact every day. And the more they interact with each other, the more they accept each other. Encouraging people of different generations, race, and income levels to mingle and share common space is a positive experience. Through this experience they learn that they can peacefully coexist with people who are different from themselves.

Densification is happening in Philadelphia, Washington, D.C., Boston— in most cities, actually. Even sprawled-out cities like Austin, Texas, are densifying, with tall residential towers downtown. Unfortunately, they don't have the shared street life to create the experience of the city yet, but that will come.

In Philadelphia just go to Rittenhouse Square, where you can see all strata of society. There are homeless people next to people who walked out of million-dollar condos. The place is balanced and respectful, as the world should be.

Mark A. Focht is a registered landscape architect, first deputy commissioner of Philadelphia Parks and Recreation, and president of the American Society of Landscape Architects (2013–2014).

→
Rittenhouse Square, Philadelphia

DUCHA HALO
JIA YOU

Provide a warm shower and reduce the spread of illness.

———

Ducha Halo is a portable shower made from easily obtainable and inexpensive parts available at any hardware store. It can be made for around seventeen dollars and is easily assembled. A DIY kit includes a simple pump, valves, and hoses that yield a fifteen-minute-long hand shower, with water heated over coals.

This shower is not for people who have access to running water. It came out of Safe Agua Chile—the first collaboration between Designmatters at Art Center College of Design and Chile's Un Techo para mi País—which was aimed at creating new ideas for water usage in a Santiago slum.

The teachers and students who engaged the Safe Agua project went to a Chilean slum to conduct intensive field research. They saw many water problems related to bathing, cooking, and laundry.

Team Ducha Halo saw that the comfort of a simple hot shower is out of reach for many people around the world. This affects people's health, hygiene, and self-esteem. The team designed this affordable, pressurized system to provide a warm shower and reduce the spread of illness while using less than the amount of water used in traditional showers.

Seeing this was a turning point for me: I didn't know that design could make such a meaningful impact for people in need.

Jia You is a retail and brand designer at Gensler LA.

→
Ducha Halo, Safe Agua project, Chile

ECO-LODGES
AZIZA CHAOUNI

Create models that mix old and new; they will be better accepted.

___

My inspiration for the future is a journey I took across the Sahara Desert. I received a traveling fellowship from Harvard University to explore eco-lodges across the countries in the Saharan region. I wondered, how can a building be sustainable in the middle of the desert with no water or electricity? I researched local architecture, met with craftsmen and builders, traveled from Morocco to Egypt, and visited Jordan, which has exemplary case studies.

The eco-lodges I visited had unique architectural strategies that blend the local language with new technologies and systems. Some were made of earth, others out of mud bricks. But they weren't just beautiful and intelligent buildings: they were made to survive in an environment that has nothing for you.

They respond to our basic needs without affecting the environment. They are in remote areas, but most importantly they have a symbiotic relationship with the surrounding areas. With some, mechanical and even sewage systems helped restore part of the landscape. In others, the landscape itself was used as thermal mass.

Each offered simple but effective lessons: use solar chimneys, catch the wind and run it through the floor or walls, orient yourself in terms of the sun, use traditional percentages for building openings. Each side of a building—east, west, north, south—has clear rules for the local craftspeople. Of course, they had no access to LEED consultants. Their designs are rooted in reality, in common sense.

We can also adapt the local architecture and bring it into our contemporary lifestyles. These buildings don't have to be just for tourists; they can be for locals, too. Eco-lodges can be a model for modern lifestyles in Arab countries.

I'm from Morocco. In the developing world, what's old is often seen as backward and should be discarded in favor of what's new. If we want these sustainable older models to be accepted, we need hybrid models that mix old and new, since people want to live in a contemporary way. These eco-lodges did just that.

Aziza Chaouni is founding principal of Aziza Chaouni Projects and assistant professor at the John H. Daniels Faculty of Architecture, Landscape, and Design at the University of Toronto.

→
Feynan Eco-lodge, Jordan

EL PORVENIR SOCIAL KINDERGARTEN
BARRY BERGDOLL

Belong to the whole community.

———

New research is blurring the borders between architecture, landscape, and urbanism. A lot of this is being labeled sustainable, but it occurred to me that not all of it actually is. Beyond environmental sustainability, we also have to focus on social sustainability. Some projects have excellent intentions, but they are not sustainable if they can't be maintained.

In a neighborhood in transition in Bogotá, Colombia, the architect Giancarlo Mazzanti created a kindergarten based on how a community relates to itself. It was built through a collaborative design process with the community and is also a result of its natural environment.

The kindergarten is in El Porvenir, an extremely poor area. It's a brilliant design. It looks informal, like a bunch of children's blocks—colorful cubes in a loose village— inside a perfectly ringed perimeter that allows for transparency from the outside. It's not hidden away.

The kindergarten can be open or closed at certain physical points. It can be used around the clock. At night, it becomes a community center. There are activities from early morning until evening. This is a place that belongs to the whole community.

Most playgrounds are not places where adults want to spend time. But Mazzanti and the community solved that challenge. Their kindergarten is an exemplar of social sustainability.

Barry Bergdoll is professor at Columbia University and curator at the Museum of Modern Art in New York.

→

El Porvenir Social Kindergarten, Bogotá, Colombia

EMSCHER PARK
ALAN M. BERGER

**Transform industrial wastelands
into parks.**

———

The project that gives me hope about the
future impact of landscape architecture is
Emscher Park in the Ruhr Valley of Germany.
This place was the epicenter of the German
steel industry during the twentieth century.
The valley's industrial legacy has now been
turned into an eight-hundred-square-mile
(2,072 sq. km) regional park system bounded
by two rivers.

This is one of the few contemporary
parks developed in an industrial waste site,
comprehensively and at the regional scale. It's
also one of the few parks that survived twenty
years of planning, through several political
regimes. The entire Ruhr Valley has become
this one huge, amazing project.

While many people know about Duisburg
Nord, which revamped a steel plant and
turned it into a garden park, the larger
Emscher Park in which it sits is much more
fascinating and diverse, and rips open tired
landscape paradigms.

*Alan M. Berger is professor of landscape
architecture and urban design at the
Massachusetts Institute of Technology.*

↗
Indoor Ski Slope, Emscher Park, Germany

ENDING ALARM FATIGUE
HUGH LIVINGSTON

Apply the niche hypothesis to our healing environments.

―――

Our lives are filled with beeping machines, often communications without nuance, and consequently are lost amid the noise of our surroundings. My German car is no less expressive when communicating "low washer fluid" than for "engine on fire," conditions for which my own response might vary. An office building I visited had nineteen beeping sounds, taking me from the garage to the forty-third-floor desk. Many of these sounds are redundant: the elevator beeps its arrival at each floor while announcing the floor number in a human voice.

Dr. Bernie Krause, equal parts musician and avian bio-acoustician, is studying birdsong around the world. He became aware of spectral separations among cohabiting populations in a biome, almost as if they were avoiding competition in acoustic space, singing higher and lower than neighboring members of other species. This became known as the Niche Hypothesis, and it turns out to be true in the temporal domain as well as in frequency. It's a simple but elegant premise that suggests ways to have sound sources coexist in the same space, without competing, using amplitude as the only dimension.

This is an approach we can use in the most taxing—and critical—of auditory environments: today's high-technology hospital, where alarms constantly require attention (1,100 per day per patient, in one recent study).

A project that surely represents a hope for sustainability in sound design is under way at the University of California, San Francisco, School of Nursing, in conjunction with leading medical equipment manufacturer GE Healthcare. It's an attempt to reduce what has become known in the medical environment as alarm fatigue. We certainly can hope that these innovations will have applications in all aspects of our lives, making for more efficient communication between machine and human.

Hugh Livingston is an artist who adapts ecological sources for the creation of visual and sonic environments.

→
Hospital monitors

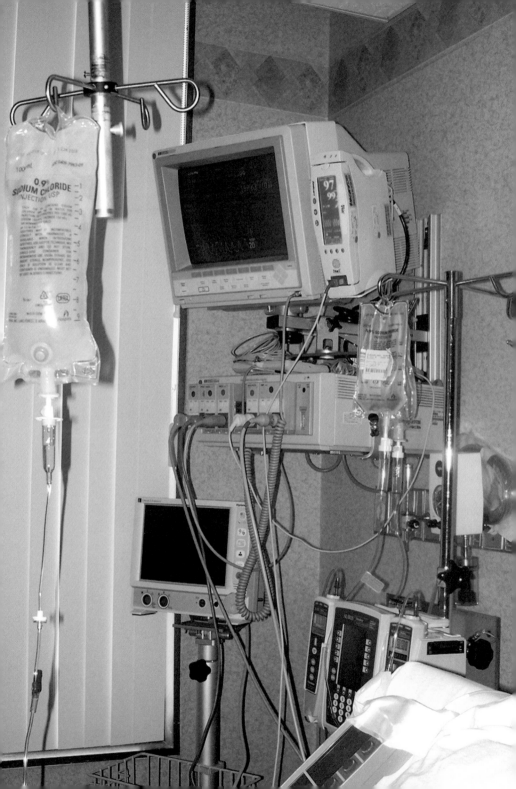

ESTUAIRE
MARC ARMENGAUD

Use public art to create a platform for environmental preservation.

Saint-Nazaire, at the mouth of La Loire estuary, is a major harbor where there are refineries, shipbuilding facilities, and warehouses. Nantes, at the end of the estuary and thirty-seven miles (60 km) from the Atlantic Ocean, is the sixth-largest city in France. Nantes and Saint-Nazaire are deeply interconnected yet separate cities. There is sprawl between the two, which has become a critical environmental issue.

The curator Jean Blaise created Estuaire, an art biennale, to ask the question: How can we bring these two cities together? He realized that their only real connection is their landscape: the estuary.

The biennale had three episodes, in 2007, 2009, and 2012. Permanent artworks now sit on both banks of the river between the cities. The artists looked at this strange landscape stuck between two cities and collaborated with local inhabitants to make sense of the place. The artworks created a platform for actors—industrialists, unions, environmental organizations, scientists, fishermen, and many others—to come together. They all shared a common ambition but, in the end, gave their vision over to the artists.

Well-known contemporary artists from around the world contributed works, including Erwin Wurm, Tadashi Kawamata, Gilles Clément, and Felice Varini. Artworks include a wooden, handmade observatory in the marsh; the metal skeleton of a dragon fighting the open sea; a secret garden growing from what wind carries onto the concrete roof of an old German submarine bunker; a Jurassic collection of huts and micropublic spaces designed with schoolkids; and a water tower with a floating house on top that can be rented as a hotel room.

The artists incubated a new identity for the area based on emptiness. The goal was to reveal the presence of the estuary, which connects everyone.

The result was that everyone became aware of the environment they need to protect and that we need to preserve this unique landscape precious for its biodiversity. The estuary zone is now a thirty-seven-mile-long by twenty-four-mile-wide (60 km by 40 km) park shaped by a comprehensive strategy that covers tourism, recreation, and natural preservation.

This effort was not the classic top-down approach of a politician or designer, or the classic participatory bottom-up one. The project made a huge blind spot visible, creating a new platform for action. Everyone—some trying to preserve the environment and some trying to destroy it—teamed up around the dynamics that the biennale created. And the art contributed to a massive transformation of that reality. It's not a recipe for every place, but it provides some insights.

Marc Armengaud is founding member and director of the AWP office for territorial reconfiguration.

→
(clockwise from top left) *Les Anneaux* by Daniel Buren; *Villa Cheminée* by Tatzu Nishi; *Le Jardin des Orpins et des Graminées* by Gilles Clément; and *Le Pendule* by Roman Signer, all contemporary artworks at Estuaire Art Biennale, Nantes and Saint-Nazaire, France

FREIBURG
MARCUS VEERMAN

Meet people's social, physical, and emotional needs.

———

Freiburg is a community in southwest Germany that is striving toward complete sustainability. It has a whole suburb built on sustainable principles. It was created out of a movement supported by all levels of government and community.

When I think of all the projects labeled as sustainable—a sustainable café or business—that's all fantastic, but they are usually part of broader systems that are not sustainable, like energy or transportation networks. Freiburg is a change from both the usual bottom-up and top-down approaches in community, industry, and government.

One housing development in Freiburg is a high-density apartment complex. Its roof is entirely covered in solar cells. Windows point toward the sun, which saves energy and makes people feel good. Everyone in the complex has a private balcony and garden. The homes are connected to good-quality public transportation and walkways and bike paths. Walkers and cyclists are protected with separate paths and laws that actively restrict car access and speed. There are lots of outdoor spaces around the apartment buildings. People can use the space to grow vegetables, play with their kids, and have a barbeque.

In normal communities, the front door of a building faces the road. Here, the front door faces a pedestrian and bike lane, and pocket parks are dispersed through the community.

When you step outside, there's a path that encourages biking, walking, and public transport.

Freiburg filled in an abandoned concrete quarry with water and created a park and community environmental center. I'm not sure why we don't do this more often, but the city also planted fruit trees in the park and built wire and wood structures for grapevines. The park combines social and edible spaces.

The community in Freiburg is focused on what is important. It has achieved a good balance. Freiburg tries to meet people's social, physical, and emotional needs sustainably.

Some examples of environmental sustainability can seem a little austere. If we are too focused on energy and resource conservation at all costs, we end up sacrificing other things we need to thrive. Freiburg shows us that real sustainability is closely related to our happiness and well-being, and that's what we all want.

Marcus Veerman is founder and CEO of Playground Ideas, which has given 250,000 children in the developing world access to time and space for play.

↗
Freiburg, Germany

FRUITVALE VILLAGE
LISA RICE

Merge community with opportunity.

———

Fruitvale Village in Oakland, California, was developed in the 1990s by the nonprofit organization Unity Council. I visited and was amazed by all the novel ideas put in place that merge community with opportunity. I'm all about expanding opportunity for neighborhoods that have been disenfranchised or isolated. Fruitvale is an interconnected, open, well-planned development that has become a national model for livable communities.

There is a Bay Area Rapid Transit (BART) station near Fruitvale. The Unity Council cooperated with the BART system and local and state government to ensure that neighborhood residents had clear access to the station.

The Unity Council had a 360-degree design strategy; it's a well-thought-out mixed-use development. As a result, Fruitvale has better access to jobs, transportation, educational opportunities, and beautiful green spaces. There is an affordable housing component, which is extremely important—particularly for regions like the Bay Area, which have high rents. And the Unity Council designed the community to incorporate services, too.

There are easily accessible day care and retail businesses that are important to community members. In Phase II of Fruitvale Village, the Unity Council will continue its revitalization of the area to bring in new residents and home ownership opportunities.

Place really does matter. Where you live determines so much about how you live your life. That is why it is important to have places like Fruitvale Village. It is a shining example of how communities can be planned to be thriving and inclusive, and provide opportunities for all residents.

Lisa Rice is vice president for the National Fair Housing Alliance.

→
Fruitvale Village, Oakland, California

GENERAL MILLS SCULPTURE GARDEN
KONGJIAN YU

**Root design in ecology; it has
a beautiful form.**

———

The General Mills Sculpture Garden
designed by Michael Van Valkenburgh is
a project that had a huge impact on me
when I was becoming a landscape architect,
and on my way to understanding ecological
landscapes. Since then, it has remained
a reference point for me.

In front of a Modernist glass building,
the garden was a patch of designed nature,
a sparse birch forest with native grasses
and wildflowers under the trees. It was
a tiny project. Natural meadows have evolved
with seasonal fires, so Van Valkenburgh's
meadow was actually set on fire, according
to the season. In 2000 General Mills
demolished it for some unknown reason,
but I still consider it a keystone project
for my professional career.

The garden tested how to use designed
nature, in both form and process. It's a
minimalist landscape ecologically rooted.
The garden showed us that ecology has
a beautiful form. But the project was also
designed with a real human vision and
sense of aesthetic value. It's deeply rooted
in the cultural context of the region, too.

The project demonstrated that the role
of landscape architecture is separate from
architecture—in that landscape architecture
has its own identity and its own form, and is
not simply an extension of the building.
In this case, the garden was a figure of its
own, with the building as background.

The garden became more valuable to me
after it was demolished. It might have gone
too far too fast, which made this garden
a pioneer. Or maybe we just destroy things
we value. In any case, the garden was a
valuable test.

*Kongjian Yu is professor and dean of
the College of Architecture and Landscape
at Peking University and president
of Turenscape.*

→

General Mills Sculpture Garden, Minneapolis,
Minnesota

GRAND PARIS
NICOLAS BUCHOUD

Take action at the regional level; it can be efficient and meaningful.

———

While visitors often declare their eternal flame for Paris "in spring" or "with my wife," most don't realize how serious it has become here since the suburban riots in 2005 that paralyzed the Paris metropolitan region for a month. Visitors likewise ignore that this can happen in their own cities, and there are common lessons we can learn.

In recent history Paris and its surroundings have been shaped by three eras, occurring roughly every forty years. Heavy industry and railway urbanization began in the late nineteenth century. Then, the constitutional consensus that rose near the end of World War II in 1944–1945 defined the long-term rules of a state-run society. Finally, there was the late-1960s regional planning and transportation framework. It seems that we have reached the end of the last forty-year cycle, with a globalized urban future.

I think this is why the Grand Paris process initiated in 2007 by the former French president so rapidly gained momentum. The process of rethinking the future of the Paris region through a pragmatic urban and environmental approach has turned into a successful narrative beyond initial expectations.

A mix of investments in infrastructure, innovation, and sustainability, the Grand Paris plan relieves us of the heavy burden of institutional complexity. The plan restored a sense that taking action at the large scale can be both efficient and meaningful.

Our collective ability to understand how we live and to bring adequate responses to global and local challenges alike gives me hope for the future. Urban affairs should be no longer about jurisdictional fights, but about building the future for the next generation.

Cities have historically been places for knowledge and freedom. They must be the engines of freedom and progress in the twenty-first century. Grand Paris has paved the way.

My hope is that we have the courage to continue building coalitions strong enough to reset institutional arrangements, so we can shape our lives, leverage local development opportunities with global capital, and develop new human resources.

Nicolas Buchoud is founding principal of Renaissance Urbaine in France.

→
Locals and Tourists #4 (GTWA #3): Paris

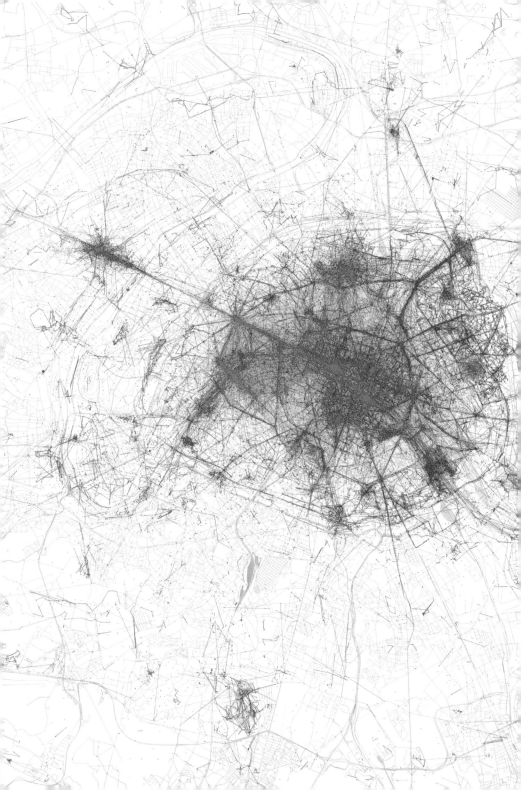

GREEN CITY, CLEAN WATERS
INGA SAFFRON

Use parks to create places people want to hang out in and manage storm water at the same time.

___

Philadelphia's claim to fame is the water department's new progressive storm water management plan. My shorthand for it is "parks, not pipes."

Basically, the city came to realize it would cost about a bazillion dollars to update its antiquated combined sewer system to handle increased storm water flow. The city is under a federal mandate to reduce its overflows into rivers when it rains heavily. Moreover, Philadelphia has a real shortage of green space. So it combined these two ideas: Instead of building twenty-five-inch (63 cm) pipes, they will use green spaces to absorb rainwater. It is the most sustainable thing that Philadelphia is doing.

I really like the idea of low-tech, low-cost ways to deal with an environmental problem, because the question is always, how do we pay for it? Those long, big pipes cost a billion dollars, and a city like Philadelphia doesn't have that kind of money, nor does the federal government. Using parks to manage storm water is passive in a good way. It brings many good values together.

Cities like Philadelphia are also repopulating, which is better for sustainability. With more urban parks, people will be more willing to give up that backyard in the suburbs. It's a win-win: we can give people nice places to hang out in that also manage storm water.

Philadelphia is not as threatened as some coastal cities facing rising sea levels, but keeping the edge of our rivers green and parklike will also help mitigate the effects of a rise in water levels.

The city is creating other win-wins. Many schools have been paved over to create parking spaces for teachers. There is now a movement to break up all that asphalt and make these places green and permeable. That push has happened because we need to deal with the storm water. The storm water management plan just pulls in so many issues of the moment.

The city is also rewriting design regulations to require every development over one hundred thousand square feet (9,200 sq. m) to responsibly capture water on-site. Businesses and developers freaked out over the new rules but have since calmed down and gotten creative about how they meet the standards, with new green roofs, cisterns, and reusing wastewater in toilets.

The more it happens, the more it becomes the norm.

Inga Saffron is the Pulitzer Prize–winning architecture critic for the Philadelphia Inquirer.

↗
Hawthorne Park, Philadelphia

GREEN INFRASTRUCTURE
DIANA BALMORI

Green our infrastructure to make us more adaptable.

———

After the devastation of Hurricane Sandy, the U.S. Army Corps of Engineers announced it will work throughout the nation with only soft, green infrastructure, as opposed to creating new hard infrastructure—concrete, steel, walls, pipes—which has been its modus operandi since the nineteenth century. The Corps of Engineers is now looking to living systems as a way to improve the resiliency of American coastlines.

This new direction was announced by a Corps engineer in a presentation to ten design teams selected by the U.S. Department of Housing and Urban Development through its Rebuild by Design competition, which aims to create models of climate-resilient design in the areas hardest hit by Sandy in New York and New Jersey.

Green infrastructure is about working with living systems instead of inert ones. These systems are based on the rhythms and particularities of natural elements, including water, vegetation, and aquatic living creatures. Green infrastructure leverages elements already found in nature and harnesses them to help us adapt to changing conditions.

The very dramatic turnaround of the Corps of Engineers can be attributed to the work of the landscape architecture profession over the past fifteen years. The field has developed a solid vocabulary of green systems, from green roofs to rain gardens and filtering ponds, and from planted streams for cleaning drainage water to paving systems that allow water to seep through. We now have the ability to engineer coastal marsh systems to protect coastlines, an example of a much-needed system, post-Sandy. These new green technologies are reflected in patent applications, as the Louisiana State University landscape architecture professor Richard Hindle has demonstrated recently in his research on patents.

Diana Balmori is founder and principal of Balmori Associates in New York City and author of A Landscape Manifesto.

→
Terraces for Marsh Creation, Sabine National Wildlife Refuge, west of Hackberry, Louisiana

GUADALUPE RIVER PARK
WES MICHAELS

**Embed design thinking in big
bureaucracies.**

The Guadalupe River Park in San Jose,
California, was a drainage canal that went
through the center of the city. The landscape
architecture firm Hargreaves Associates
convinced the U.S. Army Corps of Engineers
to rethink how it approaches these kinds of
urban waterways for the design of the park.

Instead of trying to channelize water,
like the Corps did with the Los Angeles
River, or simply beautifying the engineered
infrastructure, as it did with the San Antonio
River Walk, Hargreaves Associates convinced
the Corps to let the water open up and spread
out into the landscape. The Guadalupe River
is dry most of the year, but it experiences
flash floods during the rainy season. The
river park is a flood control project that also
provides habitat for wildlife and open
space for recreation.

This was one of the first examples of
using a "soft infrastructure" approach to
urban water systems, which is now common.
The project is also one of the first and most
well-known examples of how a landscape
architect affected the development of a major
infrastructure project, instead of following a
traditional top-down approach. Hargreaves
brought new thinking about ecology, open
spaces, and communities to the table. It
was very influential and opened up a new
dialogue in collaboration with the Corps.

It was a breakthrough that proved that
landscape architects can talk about the big
issues. The role of designers in large infrastructure projects is much more common
now. Guadalupe River Park was also a small
step for design thinking, because engineering
is a design activity by nature.

Many of our major issues are being
addressed primarily by policy initiatives
that regulate agricultural practices, clean air
and water, and climate change. The question
then becomes: How can we embed design
thinking in more of these big bureaucracies
that create policy? The U.S. Environmental
Protection Agency is trying to solve problems
through policy initiatives, but using design
thinking to reach solutions may be easier.
For example, instead of trying to solve water
quality issues along the Mississippi River
Basin through policy initiatives coordinated
between multiple states, what if we could
design a series of water-cleansing parks that,
like our National Parks, cross jurisdictional
boundaries? How are we going to bring
design thinking into these policymaking
organizations? What's going to be the next
Guadalupe River Park?

*Wes Michaels is a principal at Spackman
Mossop + Michaels and faculty member
of the Robert Reich School of Landscape
Architecture at Louisiana State University.*

↗

Guadalupe River Park, San Jose, California

THE HIGH LINE
JEFF SHUMAKER

Suspend disbelief and see the potential.

———

The High Line, an elevated park that runs through Chelsea in New York City, started with the community. In the spirit of the urban activist Jane Jacobs, it was the idea of two neighborhood residents, Joshua David and Robert Hammond, to save the structure and turn it into a park. The Bloomberg administration listened to them and saw the potential, supporting the project from the beginning.

Prior to the Bloomberg administration, neighboring property owners had wanted to demolish the High Line, which was then an abandoned railroad track leading from Gansevoort Street up to 34th Street, because they viewed it as an eyesore and an impediment to future development. But the Department of City Planning developed a mechanism whereby property owners' development rights could be transferred away from the immediate zone around the High Line to designated areas within the Special West Chelsea District, enabling them to realize the value of their land while still keeping the air and light around the High Line intact. Many don't understand that this transfer of property rights is really what allowed the High Line to happen.

The High Line eventually came out of a public-private partnership. The city covered much of the capital costs, while the Friends of the High Line organization agreed to cover the long-term maintenance costs.

This turned out to be a very good investment for the city, since it helped generate considerable residential and commercial development in the areas surrounding the High Line, which continues to this day.

As delegations from other cities and countries visit the High Line, they always ask, "How can we create our own High Line?" The answer I give is always the same: Think of something that's unique to your place, some place embedded in the fabric of your city that can have a similarly transformative effect. No other city can exactly replicate the High Line because it is specific to a particular time and place in New York.

The High Line shows us that if people want to see something happen, they can work together to make it happen. The community, city government, and property owners all worked together throughout the entire process. This can happen in other places in a transformative way.

Collaboration is about people suspending disbelief and seeing the potential. If Josh and Rob hadn't randomly met at that community meeting, formed a nonprofit, and pushed to save the High Line, it would have never happened. This shows that community still matters and that important and innovative ideas are still generated at the community level.

Jeffrey Shumaker is chief urban designer for the New York City Department of City Planning.

→
The High Line, New York

HOLDING PATTERN
JOHN PETERSON

Use local needs as material for design expression.

I'm interested in social sustainability. There has been a lot of traction around environmental sustainability, but there has been less focus on the social side. I want to look at *Holding Pattern*, an installation by Interboro Partners at MoMA PS1, the contemporary art museum in Queens, New York.

For the installation, Interboro interviewed community members and organizations to see what their needs were. It talked with the taxi drivers who gathered on a nearby corner and the neighborhood youth dance school. The taxi drivers said that they wanted shade. The dance school said that it wanted full-length mirrors. Other local groups wanted ping-pong and foosball tables and a climbing wall.

After completing interviews around the neighborhood of PS1, Interboro sat down and looked at all the desires of the community and cataloged them so they could be included as part of the installation. Each item in the installation—all the trees, furniture, mirrors, and game tables—was tagged as "owned" by the group it was destined to go to. And then, when the installation was over, the items were distributed to the local groups in need.

Holding Pattern had a highly effective reuse strategy. There was no waste at the end of the installation. The idea of looking at what would happen after the primary use of an object is over—and then turning around and using that to generate its primary use—is interesting. We usually just create something that fits our needs and hope that sometime later it will fit someone else's.

This is the highest form of community reuse. There are people with desires in every community. We can name these desires and try to fulfill them.

The patrons of PS1 come from outside the neighborhood surrounding the museum. So serving the museum's immediate neighborhood is a new way to think about high-cultural expression.

What gives me hope is that progressive designers like Interboro could look at local, social needs as material for their design expression.

John Peterson is founder and president of Public Architecture.

→

Holding Pattern, MoMA PS1, Queens, New York

LENI SCHWENDINGER

Improve the quality of sustainable lighting.

———

I'm so excited about Illuminate—a three-year research program in six European countries financed by the European Commission—that it gives me chills. This project looked at both public and cultural city areas, from Lithuania to Ireland!

The press proselytized early compact fluorescents as the answer to all energy woes. Even the *New Yorker*'s cover in July 2007 depicted the Statue of Liberty's torch as a spiral bulb. I have a dim view of this market-driven panacea, with its toxic elements and manufacturing processes that are certainly not in line with our goals for sustainability, and the lighting quality of these bulbs and the gray horribleness they produce.

The public thinks that new light-emitting diodes (LED) are the best thing since sliced bread. But only recently have manufacturing standards been put in place so that designers can rate LED quality from several standpoints.

The Illuminate research study, which was completed in 2014, examined LED lighting systems in seven pilot sites, including urban spaces, exhibition spaces in museums, and aquariums.

The researchers—engineers, designers, and manufacturers—created criteria for measuring LED against traditional lamp sources. For example, they looked at many factors, including the amount of energy saved, which reduces carbon dioxide emissions. And they examined the quality of light, which is measured in terms of brightness, color temperature, and color rendition. Color rendition applies to whether the color of the lit object looks true to life.

It is heartening to read about good scientific methodology, in this case, leaving the lighting systems in place for twelve months before assessment. And the research found that LEDS produce a high level of energy savings: an average of 60 percent over a year.

This European project gives me hope because it's a well-funded experiment with a great geographic spread and cooperation. The findings will have a landmark effect on sustainable lighting moving forward.

It is clear that in the future, we will be able to use LEDS with intelligent controls, creating malleable lighting for our streets and public spaces.

Leni Schwendinger leads the Nighttime Design/Global Lighting Urbanist initiative at Arup, and her designs and artworks illuminating public spaces are found around the world.

→
Luminance Map, Belfast City Hall, Ireland

INHOTIM
TATIANA BILBAO

Invest in the long term through arts education.
——

Inhotim is a private foundation with a museum set in a garden. It's in a rural area near Belo Horizonte, Brazil. The foundation was created by a rich man. It has a fantastic contemporary art collection with works by all the major artists. The works were created for specific sites within the garden. It's a beautifully designed place.

Inhotim is responsible not only because of how it uses nature but also because of its ethical relationship with the surrounding community. Maintenance is done by workers from the surrounding areas. Artisans are hired from there, too. Its ambitious art education programs are for its neighboring communities, places where the arts are not a priority. Inhotim has found a way to introduce art to these communities. Art raises our nature.

More and more, the people who hold the majority of capital in the world must build responsible projects with their money. Inhotim is not about simply giving money away but also about educating people for the long term. Inhotim gives us the tools we need for a better future.

Tatiana Bilbao is principal of the Mexico-based firm Tatiana Bilbao S.C.

↗
Inhotim, Brazil

KHOO TECK PUAT HOSPITAL
TIMOTHY BEATLEY

Design hospitals to be community centers.

———

Khoo Teck Puat Hospital in Singapore is a biophilic building with a great abundance of green elements. It's a hospital in a garden.

Singapore is known as the garden city; its new motto is "We are a city in the garden." It believes everyone should aspire to live in a garden environment, surrounded by nature, and that every piece of empty land should be filled with nature. More than any other city, Singapore is also thinking vertically, creating buildings filled with nature.

Liak Teng Lit, the CEO of the Khoo Teck Puat Hospital, wanted a building where your heart rate and blood pressure go down as you enter. Hospitals are inherently stressful. You are there because you anticipate an operation or worse. Instead of stressing patients and visitors out, he built a hospital that acts as a partner in the healing process.

Patients look out onto multiple layers of green roofs, planter boxes along the windows, and a courtyard garden. There is a set of healing spaces with a waterfall connected by water spaces and fishponds, which provide habitats to many species of fish.

One green roof is actually a dramatic urban farm where patients can watch food being grown and harvested. When Lit surveyed the patients to discover what they thought of the farm, they said, "We love watching it, we love seeing food being grown."

The building is an ark designed to partly restore lost nature. The hospital's level of success is judged in terms of how many bird and butterfly species the gardens attract.

The hospital is also a community center. In the United States, hospitals are high security, but this hospital attracts people from the neighborhood. Local students come here to study, and it acts as a park as well.

This place makes me hopeful because it shows how health care facilities can be designed to include nature. While there is no recorded evidence, my gut feeling is that this building does heal. This is a hospital that people want to be in.

Timothy Beatley is the Teresa Heinz Professor of Sustainable Communities at the University of Virginia.

→
Khoo Teck Puat Hospital, Singapore

THE LEICHTAG FOUNDATION RANCH
MIA LEHRER

Provide a way out of poverty and protect communities from sprawl at the same time.

———

The Leichtag Foundation owns a seventy-acre (4,046 sq. m) ranch in Encinitas, a town near San Diego, California. It uses this ranch to teach Jewish values of self-sufficiency through agriculture. It seeks to heal the Earth through service.

The ranch, which reflects the rich agricultural history in this peri-urban area, is land-banked, protecting it from becoming more single-family homes. It's now at the forefront of thinking about high-performance agriculture. The foundation brings young fellows in and exposes them to food justice issues through policy lectures, conferences, and retreats.

With urban densification, we now have major problems with food and sustainability. We can't produce food within our own communities while cities continue to rapidly sprawl, and so much of California's produce is grown for other communities rather than local ones. There is no support for these kinds of farmers. California's huge farms produce 50 percent of the country's produce but only keep 2 percent; the other 50 percent is then imported from South America at great cost to America's local farms.

The Leichtag Foundation's ranch teaches the value of community-based food production. The young students at the ranch are the next generation of California's local farmers. They need to see farming as a respectable profession.

The ranch is becoming a cluster of exciting activity: a new green school will be built, and there will be a farmer's market with permanent food stalls for local vendors, making it a much more attractive business platform for them. The adjacent San Diego Botanical Garden is putting in a new sustainability center, too.

This agricultural land could have been sold off for development. Here, like everywhere, farming is moving farther and farther away from our cities. The Leichtag Foundation is helping ensure that farming remains a part of local communities and can continue to provide a way out of poverty.

Mia Lehrer is founder and principal at Mia Lehrer + Associates in Los Angeles.

→
Leichtag Foundation Ranch and environs, San Francisco

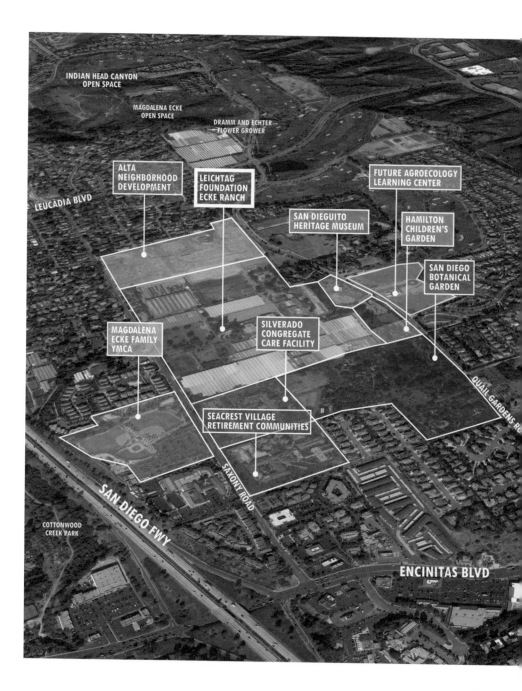

INDIAN HEAD CANYON
OPEN SPACE

MAGDALENA ECKE
OPEN SPACE

DRAMM AND ECHTER—
FLOWER GROWER

ALTA
NEIGHBORHOOD
DEVELOPMENT

LEICHTAG
FOUNDATION
ECKE RANCH

FUTURE AGROECOLOGY
LEARNING CENTER

LEUCADIA BLVD

SAN DIEGUITO
HERITAGE MUSEUM

HAMILTON
CHILDREN'S
GARDEN

SAN DIEGO
BOTANICAL
GARDEN

MAGDALENA
ECKE FAMILY
YMCA

SILVERADO
CONGREGATE
CARE FACILITY

QUAIL GARDENS Rd

SEACREST VILLAGE
RETIREMENT COMMUNITIES

SAN DIEGO FWY

SAXONY ROAD

COTTONWOOD
CREEK PARK

ENCINITAS BLVD

THE LIGHTNING FIELD
J. MEEJIN YOON

Think more deeply about our environment.

———

Walter De Maria's *The Lightning Field* in New Mexico marks the space in a way that is conscious of the landscape. It has a minimal footprint. But *The Lightning Field* also shows us that we can have a relationship with the environment.

The Lightning Field is not about excavating materials but about harnessing existing elements in the atmosphere. It shows us that energy is literally in the air around us.

This artwork teaches us by moving us. It translates the environment into a phenomenon that has a powerful emotional response. It asks us to think more deeply about our environment.

J. Meejin Yoon is professor and head of the Department of Architecture at the Massachusetts Institute of Technology, founder of MY Studio, and cofounder of Höweler + Yoon Architecture LLP.

→
Walter De Maria, *The Lightning Field*, 1977.
Western New Mexico. Courtesy Dia Art Foundation, New York. Photo: John Cliett

LION'S PARK PLAYSCAPE
MIKYOUNG KIM

Integrate environmental and social awareness into design.

Lion's Park Playscape in Greensboro, Alabama, was designed and built by students of the Rural Studio, an off-campus collaborative design-build program at Auburn University that was started by two professors, Samuel Mockbee and D. K. Ruth.

I remember attending a lecture by Mockbee, who believed that "everyone—rich or poor—deserves a shelter for the soul." As a twenty-one-year-old graduate design student, I was inspired to hear him talk about how design can change people's lives and about the importance of integrating social consciousness into the designed world we live in.

Lion's Park Playscape uses simple, recycled materials chosen based on the local climate, but it's also a very sophisticated design. Recycled fifty-five-gallon galvanized drums are arranged in a modular system to create cellular forms to play on. The drums also create a canopy that provides shade for kids during the summer. Kids totally love this place because there is so much to explore, from sound tubes to hide-and-seek mazes.

Lion's Park, like everything created by Rural Studio, was designed and built through a collaborative approach with the students and faculty. Its projects thrive on bare-bones budgets, building homes with as little as $20,000; it's very much like Habitat for Humanity, but with zing!

Kids are taught the value of sustainability in school through slogans like "reduce, reuse, recycle." Rural Studio does this and more by using innovative design as a way to signal new social awareness. Each project is shaped by the materials at hand and old-fashioned community ethics.

With Rural Studio, young designers learn about the places where they build and engage the communities they serve while offering a lively rebuke to the traditionally desolate architecture of poverty. When environmental and social awareness are integrated into design, surprising and magical experiences can emerge.

Lion's Park Playscape exudes a soulful, regenerative message: We are not separate from the natural cycles of the world but part of them. This sensible and pragmatic model for sustainability is being applied one community at a time by this collaborative design group, offering a model for the future that is hopeful and ecological.

Mikyoung Kim is an award-winning landscape architect.

→

Lion's Park Playscape, Greensboro, Alabama

LOCAL CODE / REAL ESTATES
KELLER EASTERLING

Turn cities' empty lots into a new immune system.

———

Nicholas de Monchaux's Local Code / Real Estates project has been indexing remnant properties in San Francisco and other cities across the United States. He sees all the empty, publicly owned urban lots as a new infrastructure that can be repurposed as a network.

He indexed all the empty public properties in San Francisco and discovered there are more than fifteen hundred locations. These largely correspond with parts of the city that have some economic or environmental trouble. In New York City he found that if you put all the empty public spaces together, the area would be comparable with Central Park.

De Monchaux doesn't think that these remnant public spaces should just be turned into parks. He sees them as connective tissue. He calls for land-banking them, saving them from future development, and creating a parallel market for them, as they can be useful in noncommercial ways.

These leftover spaces could be used for energy production, storm water remediation, or sewer or electrical upgrades. De Monchaux sees them as a kind of "distributed immune system." I think of them as a lymph system for the city, carrying away the bad stuff or adapting to change.

These spaces are not monolithic. They can provide another kind of system in the city. They could be traded and used for the public good, not monetized.

I like the idea of using sites to create a parallel market of value. These are ragged little spaces. They currently aren't valued at all, but they are assets, outside the trafficked mortgage products of real estate. Because they don't have these values, they make possible another system based simply on spatial attributes.

Architects know how to handle such banks of space. In a world driven by econometrics, here is a market that designers know how to shape and improve.

Keller Easterling is an architect, urbanist, and writer. Her most recent book is Extrastatecraft: The Power of Infrastructure Space.

→
NYC Local Code

LONDON CONGESTION PRICING
ANJALI MAHENDRA

Reduce carbon emissions, noise, and traffic accidents from vehicles.

———

A game-changing urban policy for me was congestion fees in the central business district of London in 2003. This policy redefined how people perceive the true costs of transportation and allowed them to make more informed choices about their modes of travel.

The initially unpopular policy was implemented by Mayor Ken Livingstone under his manifesto of "getting London moving." The goal was to manage heavy congestion in the London Central Business District (CBD). Traffic had led to gridlocked streets, negative impacts on the urban environment, and lost economic productivity. The congestion is caused by many travelers driving cars at peak hours without realizing that they in fact cause the congestion that imposes delays on themselves and other travelers, so the policy charges a fee to drivers in the CBD during periods of high traffic.

This form of pricing is also called area-wide pricing. The fee may vary by time of day or vehicle type. Although congestion reduction is often the primary objective, cities also seek to reduce emissions, noise, and traffic accidents, and to improve pedestrian access and enjoyment of public spaces and businesses.

In London, travel times decreased by 14 percent after implementation, peak period bus ridership increased by 40 percent, and there was a 20–30 percent reduction in private vehicles entering the charging zone as people shifted to other travel times or routes. The revenues from the congestion charge help fund public transportation, creating improved travel alternatives for the majority of people, rather than the minority who actually use cars in London.

Area-wide pricing has existed in some form in Singapore since 1975. In 2007 area-wide pricing was proposed in New York City, but was not approved by the state legislature.

Political will makes the London example extremely important. It was the first time that a major city with a democratically elected government implemented a relatively radical policy that has lasted for over a decade, through successive changes of government. Other city leaders around the world have followed suit.

In Asia, where vehicle fleets are doubling almost every seven to ten years because of increasing urbanization and economic growth, a policy like this is much needed to avoid the severe costs of growing motorization that people don't perceive.

Anjali Mahendra is strategy head for research and practice at EMBARQ India.

→

London Congestion Pricing

MAISON DUFORT
NATHALIE JOLIVERT

Preserve culture and traditions.

———

Gingerbread Houses were built in Haiti in the late nineteenth and early twentieth centuries by Haitian architects who studied in France. Gingerbread Houses were either designed completely in wood or used bricks at the bottom and wood on top, with cross-bracing structures to counter lateral forces. These buildings have high ceilings with multiple doors and porches that allow for ventilation in the tropical climate. Their name derives from their very ornate and colorful wood latticework.

The Gingerbread Houses survived the devastating 2010 earthquake better than the modern concrete buildings, because there's not enough local knowledge about how to properly use concrete. The Foundation for Knowledge and Liberty (FOKAL) bought Maison Dufort, a Ginger-bread House designed by the architect Léon Mathon and severely damaged by the earthquake, in order to restore and preserve it with contemporary methods.

Maison Dufort is being restored through a collaboration with local masons and experts from Belgium and California. FOKAL is reaching out to young Haitians still in school—those uninfluenced by current methods—to teach them lost skills like how to properly lay a brick by reusing old bricks from collapsed buildings as well as fabricate new bricks and create an industry, something that hasn't existed in Haiti for years. Haiti had a very repressive dictatorship, and many of the older folks with knowledge of those skills left, so they were not passed down to younger generations.

Maison Dufort is located in a district of Port-au-Prince called "Bois-Verna" that many are trying to preserve. But many of these old Gingerbread Houses that need work are inhabited by families with little money, and restoring these buildings is very expensive.

Preserving Maison Dufort gives me hope, because it's really about preserving our culture and traditions. Haiti has always been a bridge between multiple cultures. The Gingerbread Houses were influenced by European Victorian houses, but they are infused with Haitian history with their bright colors and the inclusion of Vaudou symbols in the wood latticework.

Sustainable architecture is an extension of a culture. It's not just about being shel-tered. There's a dancer who lives and teaches in a Gingerbread House in Bois-Verna. As you see dancers practicing in her home, you see a performance in a place just filled with Haiti's culture.

Nathalie Jolivert is architectural designer at Studio Drum Collaborative in Port-au-Prince, Haiti.

→

Maison Dufort, Port-au-Prince, Haiti

MALMÖ
BERT GREGORY

Get the hardware and software right.

———

A wonderful example of a contemporary place dealing with sustainable life is Malmö, Sweden. Malmö is one of the first sustainable districts that works at the level of a neighborhood. Malmö combines all types of sustainable systems—food, transportation, water, and energy—with community diversity and architectural character. It's also a beautiful place, spiritually uplifting.

As we work together to green the planet, we must look to projects like Malmö. We must figure out how to bring this model to the market-based environment of the United States.

Malmö works sustainably on multiple levels. It was a redevelopment of an industrial brownfield site: the developers repurposed land that had been ecologically damaged, reusing it instead of tapping an undeveloped greenfield site. This increases density through the redevelopment of existing sites without growing outward.

There is a sophisticated transportation system. With high-speed train access, there is hardly any need for cars, and so there are very walkable, bikeable streets.

There is an advanced system for the treatment of water, and the city is careful about water consumption. The management of storm water is naturally based. These systems are inspiring and lovely. All that vegetation provides wildlife habitat, too.

There is a comprehensive energy strategy. The city has an ambitious goal of using 100 percent renewable energy, a milestone that we should all strive to reach as rapidly as possible. Wind power is supplemented by arrays of photovoltaic panels.

The place is architecturally beautiful. There is a real character to the development. The patterns of the old repurposed industrial land are there; it feels like the old Malmö, but the old forms are also reinterpreted in new ways. The architectural diversity makes it an inspiring place, easy to love. I can see it enduring for hundreds of years.

There is a sophisticated system for capturing organic waste and turning it into biogas. One hundred percent of organics become biogas, displacing fossil fuels.

There are free lunches for all school children, and they are served totally organic foods. Fossils fuels have been removed from the food, too.

Malmö is a fair-trade city, with everything organic and ethically labeled. This shows how a society can influence the future.

Malmö got the hardware (the infrastructure) and the software (the programs that influence behaviors) right. It's a comprehensive approach to planning, with tremendous public spaces and beautiful amenities that help create a community. It's a great model.

Bert Gregory is chairman and CEO of Mithun.

→

Malmö, Sweden

MANY SMALL-SCALE PROJECTS
NINA-MARIE LISTER

Form a new language of sustainability that is beautiful and legible to everyone.

———

What do you mean by a sustainable future? For me, it's the living world of ecology, the stuff of life, the relationship between living creatures and the places they inhabit. It means that we need to understand our landscapes and the places that sustain us.

A sustainable future is one in which we have the capacity to adapt to ever-changing dynamic conditions. This means that humans, together with our environment, have transformative capacity.

Many small-scale projects—considered together—give us hope for the future. Systems thinking is critical to our success: it's about how things are connected, about the cumulative power of projects, and about thinking across scales, between sites, cities, and regions.

Sometimes we need leadership through policies led by governments and big projects that change our thinking—projects like NYC's Rebuild by Design, or the Ontario Greenbelt, or the Dutch Room for the River. But equally and perhaps more importantly to this thinking are the small, local projects. These are easily understandable. They take advantage of small opportunities to make simple changes and offer tangible solutions. If they fail, they fail safely, not catastrophically.

Projects need to make sense. They need to help us read the landscape and the ecologies that sustain us. One such project is the Rosa F. Keller Library in New Orleans. It is a simple storm water garden in an improbable place, at the bottom of the "bowl" of the city. It's an iris garden, but it also holds water and helps prevent flooding. Toronto's Sherbourne Common is similar: it holds, slows, and cleans water.

People can see how small projects work, and such projects can change how we act, as well as how we think. They change our landscape and our mindscape. In transforming water from a threat into an opportunity, these projects make ecological functions beautiful and legible to everyone. Seen together, many small-scale projects form a new language of sustainability that can provide elegant solutions for a productive, healthy future.

Nina-Marie Lister is associate professor of urban and regional planning at Ryerson University and visiting associate professor of landscape architecture at Harvard University's Graduate School of Design.

↗
Iris Garden, New Orleans

MEDIA TIC
DAVID GARCIA

Fully integrate new technology into building design.

———

The Media TIC building in Barcelona by the architecture firm Cloud 9 is an exhibition space, auditorium, and open media hub. The structure is a series of bridges, providing an open plan within. The structure spans from facade to facade, with 15,000 square feet (1,400 sq. m) of floor space. It's flexible and able to adapt for many different types of events. The building is a social magnet.

The building uses new technology not as a gimmick but as a new way to mitigate environmental challenges. The building fine-tunes its facades to shield itself from light and thermal heat from the sun.

On the south side, there is inflatable translucent cladding made of Ethylene Tetrafluoroethylene (ETFE), a fluorine-based plastic. This cladding holds a membrane filled with a mix of nitrogen gas and oil. When the sun is horizontal, the facade senses this. Its membrane becomes clouded and opaque to block out heat and light.

In winter, transparency is key. The membrane opens to let light and heat come through.

This technology provides a new way to regulate sunlight without insulation or heating and cooling systems. The building enriches our understanding of the building envelope.

Environmental solutions are perceived in the aesthetic of the building. It shows us how a new technology can be fully integral to the building design, not just added on at the end of the design process. This building challenges our perception of what a building is, but it also performs. It's quite stunning.

David Garcia is head of the Institute for Architecture and Technology at the Royal Danish Arts Academy in Denmark.

→
Media TIC, Barcelona

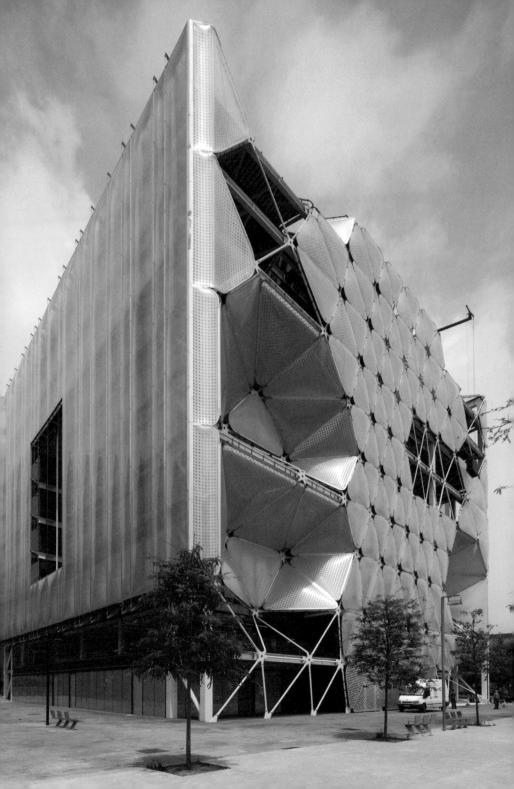

MERIAN MAP OF PARIS
EVA FRANCH I GILABERT

Involve everyone who inhabits and builds cities.

———

A map of Paris from 1616 depicts not only the city's plan but also its different inhabitants and social strata. The map shows us the city from the bottom-up and the top-down. There's the king and queen, the symbols of power next to the horizon. On the way down, we see images of merchants next to the bridges, artists, and then the workers in the fields, who constitute the base of the social economy of the city, from its center to its periphery.

This map shows us how cities are made up of all types of people and that everyone should be treated with equal attention. The first stage of sustainability is human sustainability.

In thinking about the future, we need to think about the relevant forces that should drive design. We need to involve everyone who is inhabiting, but also building, cities and territories worldwide. This is what sustainability means.

History and time are both latent in the present moment. Something one thousand years old is as old as something days old. Time is an illusion, a construction we like to believe in. Many of the deep concerns about architecture are timeless, like sustainability or ecology. These are ideas that have been around for such a long time.

Eva Franch i Gilabert is an architect and executive director and chief curator of Storefront for Art and Architecture.

→
Merian Map of Paris, by Mathaeus Merian, 1615

119

METRO LIBRARIES
ANA LUCIA GONZÁLEZ IBÁÑEZ

Build libraries where the poorest are.

———

In Medellín, Colombia, the city has built libraries for kids in subway stations. This shows me that everywhere, all the time, the city is trying to educate its children.

The library I saw is found right on the platform, as you go from one track to another. This library is in a station that connects to the metro-cable system that takes people up into the hills surrounding the city, where poor people live. This isn't a nice area.

The library is about 215 square feet (20 sq. m). The interior of the library was full, and there were about ten kids in line to get in.

The subway is the most urban environment we have—it can be so impersonal, even dangerous. The library in the station is like a pearl. It's just for kids. It completely changes the tone.

This library gives me hope for the future because it puts more good things in these kids' heads and hearts. They will now look at the city and their environment differently. They are being taught that there are other ways to see the world. These kids are our future mayors.

Medellín initiated a program of remaking the city just eighteen years ago, building a new subway and creating a network of parks and libraries. In the life of a city, eighteen years is nothing. In that time, Medellín went from a narco city ruled by drug lords to a model city. I wish more cities in Latin America had its spirit.

This is a model for other cities in Latin America. While each city is different, they share many of the same problems. These kids waiting in line to get into the library give me the hope I often don't have.

Ana Lucia González Ibáñez is director of Taller Patrimonio & Metrópoli.

→
Santo Domingo Metro Station Library, Medellín, Colombia

THE MIDTOWN GREENWAY
PETER HARNIK

Reuse rail infrastructure, our country's astonishing feat of engineering.

———

The Midtown Greenway is in Minneapolis, Minnesota. It's a rail trail that cuts east–west across the city from the Mississippi River to the lakes. An abandoned Soo Line route, it will soon be a rail with a trail when the Hennepin County Regional Railroad Authority builds a light-rail commuter line alongside it.

The old railroad was built in a trench to not interfere with auto traffic. That trench is now good for pedestrians and bicyclists, as cross streets pass over on bridges.

The two-track line was bought in the 1990s before transit plans were finalized. An active citizen group, the Midtown Greenway Coalition, sprang into action and lobbied the agency to turn half of it over to bicyclists and walkers. Today the trail is paved and nicely landscaped and even graced with community gardens. The other track is fenced off and being held for future use.

For more than ten years, the greenway has evolved into an increasingly valuable part of Minneapolis's walking and bicycling network. The rail trail has more than one million users every year, in all seasons. It's even plowed in the winter.

In 1916 American railroad companies had laid down more than 250,000 miles (402,317 km) of railroad tracks. That was the high point. By 2014 over 100,000 miles (160,927 km) have been abandoned—that's larger than the entire U.S. interstate highway system. Whether rails-to-trails or rails-with-trails, this is a vast resource.

As far as I'm concerned, life doesn't get much better than a rail trail. It memorializes the railroad industry's astonishing feats of engineering through the bridges and tunnels, smooth grades and curves. It puts old infrastructure to great new use. It provides long ribbons of natural parkland in cities. It enables autophobic people to cycle safely for pleasure or business. In the Midwest I've seen rail trails flanked by rare prairie plants, since the corridors are among the few places that have never seen a plow. And they are used not just by bicyclists—there are also skaters, mothers with strollers, people in wheelchairs, skiers in the winter. Pretty much all smiling.

Peter Harnik is director of the Center for City Park Excellence at the Trust for Public Land and cofounder of Rails to Trails.

→
Midtown Greenway, Minneapolis, Minnesota

MUSHROOM BOARD
JONSARA RUTH

Eliminate trash and chemicals.

———

A piece of mushroom board, created by Ecovative Design in upstate New York, has sat on my desk for the past six years. It has moved from the desk in my design office to the desk at my school office and back again. This product shows how rapidly growing spores of mycelium can be used to replace Styrofoam.

Mushroom board is grown from an organic process found in nature. It can be molded into any shape or thickness. Ecovative uses vegetative waste material to create the structure for the board.

If mushrooms replaced Styrofoam, we could stop using petrochemicals to make packing materials that create tons of trash and never leave the planet. Styrofoam is not only toxic to the planet, it's also coated with chemicals that are harmful to humans. We could instead grow insulating material using the energy of the Earth.

Package insulation is a huge industry. For furniture alone, shipping bulky items across continents requires tons of packing material. What happens to these packing materials at the end? They are thrown away and create landfills. With mushroom board, packaging material could be added to gardens. At the end of its life, the material could go back to the Earth, nourishing the soil in the process.

Beyond testing this as packing material, Ecovative is experimenting with creating airtight, insulated structural walls and grown-in-place building installations. It is also looking at replacing toxic spray foams, which are horrible for human and environmental health, with a mushroom spray that could fill gaps of any shape—and it's naturally flame-retardant!

This product is very exciting, as it combines cutting-edge science, technical engineering, and manufacturing know-how. Ecovative is also approaching the rollout of these products in a smart way. It is experimenting with firms in many different industries at once, including packaging, acoustic panel, and insulation companies.

Mushroom board is about eliminating trash and chemicals. It's a return to the Earth, but in a forward-thinking way. It shows that great strides in science don't need to be artificial or synthetic.

Jonsara Ruth is assistant professor and founding director of the MFA program in interior design at Parsons the New School for Design, and she leads the Brooklyn-based design collective Salty Labs.

→
Ecovative Mushroom Board sample

NEWPORT BEACH CIVIC CENTER AND PARK
JOHN KING

**Show communities that landscapes
are more than stage sets.**

———

The recent landscape that gives me hope
for the future is one that hasn't received
much attention: the Newport Beach Civic
Center and Park, near the Pacific Ocean in
Orange County, California. It combines
a wealthy community's city hall and library
with a dozen or so acres of re-created natural
landscape. The landscape was created by
an old pro, Peter Walker, and his firm PWP
Landscape Architecture.

What I like is that it's exactly what you
don't expect in an upscale urban landscape—
a naturalistic yet artistic terrain, sustainable,
very much rooted in the topography of the
place. A creek bed, which has been there for
tens of thousands of years, is the natural spine
of the project. The landscape around it is an
almost poetic evocation of different Southern
Californian places: you've got meadows,
dunes, and forests.

Better, all this comes together in a context
with Fashion Island on one side, the ultimate
outdoor-lifestyle shopping center, and master
planned subdivisions on the other. In the
middle, along MacArthur Boulevard, spills
this swirl of landscape poetry, and beyond
that lies the ocean.

There's another design layer to it, which
is extremely contemporary and colorfully
sculptural: structural insertions, pedestrian
bridges. Instead of some simple pedestrian
bridge, there's a big, dramatic, right-angled
blue stroke across the horizon. It's a metallic
accent to the scene.

The final touch, which caused a real fuss,
is a set of eight-foot-tall rabbit sculptures,
scattered throughout, which children
can play on. The sculptures are not public
art but whimsical objects that kids respond
to and enjoy. But they didn't go through the
review process and that upset the powers who
don't like being caught by surprise. While
I drove with my daughter past the space one
day, she caught a glimpse of the rabbits, so we
pulled in. At one point, there's even a circle of
rabbits. All have different colored eyes.

Newport Beach is prosperous but
thoroughly mainstream, what Renzo Piano
would call the periphery, rather than the
city. The idea that you can insert a fantastic,
large-scale, civic terrain here suggests
that sustainable provocation can take root
anywhere. If nothing else, it's a fresh
confirmation that landscapes are more
than stage sets. They're forces that shape
how we think and how we live.

*John King is architecture and urban design
critic at the* San Francisco Chronicle.

↗
Newport Beach Civic Center and Park,
Newport Beach, California

NOS QUEDAMOS
DAMON RICH

Invest in the sustenance of people power.

———

Melrose Commons is in the South Bronx, New York. In the early 1990s residents noticed some people taking notes in the neighborhood and caught wind that the New York City planning department was creating an urban renewal plan for them. They realized that the plan meant the displacement of current residents, so they organized a nonprofit group named Nos Quedamos ("We Stay"), rallied against the plan, and authored their own vision for urban renewal. They turned the whole situation around with the help of Magnusson, an architecture and planning firm, and many others.

Sustainability is not only about technological adaptation; it's about enhancing social fabric, the patient extension and augmentation of our mutual connections, and our ability to function as a society. It's about weaving change with what people know instead of venerating it as a disruptive, violent force. We can incorporate new narratives into landscapes shaped by oppression.

Since their plan was officially adopted by the City Planning Commission in 1994, Nos Quedamos has been involved with developing over two thousand units of affordable housing with retail and community space. Some buildings have evocative names, and some have amazing colors. I was told that since many Puerto Ricans, Dominicans, and others from brightly painted places are residents, they decided that the architecture should express itself in pink and peach, like a tropical Venturi, Scott Brown.

If you go to the offices of Nos Quedamos, you can see a framed, coffee-stained pencil sketch of a plan on their wall. This plan of the neighborhood was produced near the beginning of their struggle. I love that they have memorialized it like a sacred document.

Yolanda Garcia, the founder of Nos Quedamos, passed in 2005, yet she seems to have created an organization that can last into the future. We can all create plans, but sustainable ones are an extension of a community's social fabric, people getting together and talking. Only an investment in—and dedication to—the sustenance of people's power and the extension of democracy keeps a community alive.

Damon Rich is founder of the Center for Urban Pedagogy and serves as planning director and chief urban designer for the City of Newark, New Jersey.

→
Melrose Commons, Bronx, New York

OUR KAKA'AKO
JESS ZIMBABWE

Build the community up front and invest for the long term.

Our Kaka'ako is a twenty-nine-acre project in Honolulu developed by the Kamehameha School, a charitable trust formed by the last living descendant of the Hawaiian king Kamehameha. His descendants left hundreds of thousands of acres, which were designated to be used or sold only to educate native Hawaiian children about their language and culture. The trust provides scholarships and other programs, supported by the sale of land in urban areas and developed places like Kaka'ako.

Kaka'ako is a low-lying area near the water where there were once productive fish and salt ponds. It was then zoned for industry, and ten years ago it was Honolulu's warehouse district. Kaka'ako is now filled with workforce housing, condos, retail, and commercial office space.

The school started by creating a unique sense of place and then it created housing. Artists are moving into old warehouse lofts, and each month they open their studios for a collective night market. One tenant makes great beer, so a beer garden has appeared. Cultural activities have spread through the neighborhoods' alleyways. The school has made this into a neighborhood people want to live in. I want to live there.

This trust has a long horizon. It doesn't have shareholders, banks, or investors; it is not worried about immediate profits. This place will be there in perpetuity.

Kaka'ako has turned the standard development model on its head. It's a mission-based development that proves this new concept can work. I hope that other developers will follow suit and build the community up front and invest for the long-term.

Jess Zimbabwe is founding executive director of the Urban Land Institute Daniel Rose Center for Public Leadership.

↗
Geoff Seideman, owner and head brewer of Honolulu Beerworks, recently opened in Our Kaka'ako, Hawai'i

PARK(ING) DAY
JANET ECHELMAN

Connect people, empower them.

———

I want to talk about Park(ing) Day, which was created by the group Rebar. I have a personal experience. I encountered this without knowing what it was—and it expanded my thinking about how much space we allocate for automobiles and how easily we can correct that mistake.

I was walking home along our main shopping street in Coolidge Corner, Massachusetts, and saw two parking spaces that had been transformed into mini-parklets. Someone had rolled out turf, set out potted plants and lawn chairs, and provided beverages. So I sat down instead of rushing off and started talking to other people who'd similarly stumbled on it. It was such a surprising transformation, with simple means, and it showed me the potential that even small spaces can have.

When I think about sustainability, I think about how we need noncarbon energy sources, but I also think about sustainable communities. What do humans need to be happy? What resources are already here that have untapped potential? Given a constrained environment, what is something we can do to shift the use of urban space from street parking to use for people?

Community life is a central human need. It's not an add-on. Park(ing) Day shows us a small, practical way to create micro-public spaces that bring us together and enhance our lives. I see it is spreading around the world, just by closing off one parking space for the day. It's a very low barrier for entry, yet it starts a meaningful conversation about how we allocate our valuable space. That's how it drew me in.

These small acts can gather momentum to make larger changes. If we feel connected to one another, we can become empowered to change our physical and political environment. If we feel that we can reshape our streets, we can open up other questions. This is one small way an artist or designer can participate in creating a sustainable future.

If we change ourselves—and then feel empowered to shape our world according to human values—things we previously thought impossible suddenly seem real and within our reach.

Janet Echelman is a public artist who creates monumental sculpture at the scale of buildings that respond to the forces of nature.

→
Park(ing) Day, San Jose, California

PEDESTRIAN ZONES
KIM YAO

Reuse our streets, add new layers.

In dense urban environments like New York City we must reuse infrastructure and add new layers. Places must evolve. There has been an amazing set of projects by the New York City Department of Transportation, under former transportation commissioner Janette Sadik-Khan, focused on transforming streets into pedestrian zones.

These projects introduced change into a transportation system highly resistant to change. Projects like the pedestrian mall in Times Square started in a temporary fashion to test results, but they later became permanent.

Sadik-Khan, working with the vision of former Mayor Michael Bloomberg, recaptured the streetscape for people and changed use patterns. These changes gave back public space, creating outdoor spaces that reduce traffic flow.

The transformation occurred through painting streets, adding café tables and chairs, and inserting a few bollards. The street improvements were inexpensive but had a big impact.

The new pedestrian zone in Times Square is heavily used, as is the new pedestrian area near Madison Square Park, next to the Flatiron Building. These new pedestrian spaces show that people can move through the spaces near cars safely and that there is also an appetite for a greater rethinking of streets in the city. These projects signal that it's possible to create change even in places where people thought change was impossible.

What else are we taking for granted? We need more critical thinking about our urban infrastructure.

Kim Yao is a principal at the Architecture Research Office in New York.

→
Madison Square Park (above) and Times Square (below) pedestrian plazas, New York

PRIMARY SCHOOL IN GANDO
ANDRES LEPIK

Use global knowledge to activate local resources.

———

Diébédo Francis Kéré is an architect from Burkina Faso, one of the poorest countries in sub-Saharan Africa, which also has a high rate of illiteracy. He was born in the tiny village of Gando and studied architecture in Germany. While studying, he sent money home to his family, but one day he realized that this wouldn't help in the long term. He was aware that one cause of poverty is a lack of education and decided to build a school in his home village.

Kéré collected money and saved it for the school's construction by founding a nongovernmental organization. He shocked his community when he proposed the use of clay bricks for the building material, which, until that point, had only been used for storage buildings for livestock. Given his European education, he was expected to use advanced technologies and materials. But Kéré knew that it was best to work with local materials, which have their own tradition and do not consume as much fossil fuel energy. Burkina Faso craftsmen build clay bricks with their own hands, which means that they can also maintain the buildings far into the future.

Kéré designed and constructed his first building, the elementary school in Gando, using the workforce of the whole community. The finished building has three classrooms, with a large roof to protect the walls and ceilings from sun and rain.

The school was a great success; it won the Aga Khan Award for Architecture, the highest award for architecture in the Muslim world. With the prize money Kéré built a school extension, boosting the number of students, and then built a teacher's dormitory, a library, and a women's center, where women can learn to read and write, grasp better agricultural technologies, and earn more income for their families.

Burkina Faso's Ministry of Education wants Kéré to build a high school, since Gando now has high-quality elementary school students. This gives them the opportunity to expand their education.

The holistic approach of Kéré is deeply rooted in the knowledge of specific needs and conditions of his community, local materials, and local traditions. This project revitalized the skills of local craftspeople who work with clay bricks. Those skills were dying out.

Kéré's Gando projects have a high potential to affect places far beyond the village and to become exemplary for many other rural communities in Africa and elsewhere. They show that global knowledge can activate local resources. We need both.

Andres Lepik is an author and curator of architectural exhibitions.

→

Primary School Extension, Gando, Burkina Faso

PROJECT ROW HOUSES
F. KAID BENFIELD

Revitalize old neighborhoods; they are inherently environmental.

Project Row Houses started with twenty-two abandoned shotgun houses on one-and-a-half blocks in a poor section of Houston. These are wood-frame houses in which the rooms are all lined up. You can walk straight through, since there are no hallways. About half of these houses were converted into revolving showcases for African American artists. Another set was converted into two-year residencies for young single moms to learn life and career skills in a campus-like environment. There are now some forty properties, including a new section of affordable duplexes designed with the assistance of Rice University's School of Architecture.

The project was started by the artist Rick Lowe. The houses were low cost because they were abandoned. Lowe initially used volunteer labor. He eventually used the project as the base for a community development corporation, a nonprofit developer that can raise capital, which is how the project expanded to now cover six blocks.

Project Row Houses is inspirational. It happened because of one guy with an idea who had some creative, energetic friends and a vision for the future of his community. This project shows that with a good heart and fundamental concern for our fellow man, we can do incredible things. It shows the best of the human spirit.

The project is not environmental per se, but any project that revitalizes old neighborhoods in a sound way is inherently environmental because it recycles land, buildings, and infrastructure. It is antienvironmental to have gaping holes of abandoned property in our cities.

The project has since inspired others, like Watts House Project in Los Angeles, a project that renovates wood-frame houses in the shadow of the famous Watts Towers. Each renovation is a collaboration between the resident, an artist, and an architect.

F. Kaid Benfield is a blogger and author, and special counsel for urban solutions at the Natural Resources Defense Council.

↗
Project Row Houses, Houston, Texas

REBUILDING CENTER
SARAH MINEKO ICHIOKA

**Divert reusable building material
from landfills.**

I've been fascinated by the concept of salvage ever since I was a kid: the idea that one person's scrap can become another's special find. The magic is in the matchmaking: collecting worthy old materials is not enough; you have to connect them with the people who want to reuse them.

Reuse centers for building materials have been active across the United States for decades, and I'm glad that this seems to be a growing trend. Having studied a fair number of these, my favorite by far is the ReBuilding Center in Portland, Oregon.

Founded in 1998 as part of Our United Villages, a community-based nonprofit, the ReBuilding Center provides resources that make home repairs affordable to everyone, with the goal of promoting the reuse of salvaged and reclaimed materials.

Every day, three hundred visitors come to the ReBuilding Center's warehouse to browse its ever-changing inventory, including sinks, tubs, tile, lumber, doors, windows, trim, and much more. The nearly 4,700-square-yard (4,000 sq. m) warehouse, cleverly configured and full of natural light, is a self-contained case study of elegant reuse: one facade is a patchwork of salvaged windows, another is clad in flattened metal from old HVAC systems.

The warehouse is complemented by DeConstruction Services, a sustainable alternative to conventional demolition, and ReFind Furniture, which offers a diverse line of green home furnishings. All operating expenses are covered through earned income, and excess proceeds are reinvested in community outreach work.

The ReBuilding Center diverts almost six million pounds of reusable building materials from landfills every year while creating high-quality jobs and serving as a social hub and educational resource for its local community of DIY households and small contractors.

Although Portland is a notably progressive place—fertile ground for this kind of project to flourish—the ReBuilding Center offers an impressive example whose practical components could easily be adapted to many other cities that appreciate the connections between green initiatives and social and economic resilience.

Sarah Mineko Ichioka is a cultural leader, curator, and innovator with a passion for cities and their potential.

↗
ReBuilding Center, Portland, Oregon

RIVERWALK
MARION WEISS

Use minimal means to have a huge impact.

———

Ljubljana, the capital of Slovenia, is a city where the architect Jože Plečnik optimized the cultural and infrastructural potential of the Ljubljanica River. Between 1929 and 1932 he shaped a chameleon-like urban section along the river, simultaneously structuring flood control measures and creating a parallel city along the water.

The steep section cut produces a kind of reverse fortification, with bilevel landscapes and walks that offer a place to experience the city at a slower pace. At the core of the city, vertical walls inscribed with stairs, ramps, and arcades fall one story below the streets. As the river wanders past the urban core, these walls yield to a shallower angle, broadening the width of the riverwalk with stone paved terraces and water-tolerant trees, creating multilevel walks that follow the course of the river into its ultimate natural state.

Between these urban and pastoral states, a series of weirs and bridges create landmarks along the length of the river. An element I find both brilliant and subtle is the formal calibration of water to walkways. When the river is full, only an upper-level perimeter walk offers passage; when the water level is low, it follows a slender channel, leaving four levels of parallel walkways free for strollers. This dynamically changing section accommodates natural events while satisfying our desire for strolling.

At the heart of the city, Plečnik's signature triple bridge crosses the river with a spectacle of redundant crossings and delicacy of scale more common in architectural follies than infrastructure. Together, these elements create a hardworking infrastructure with a light touch.

In one stroke, the riverwalk synthesizes competitive requirements with minimal means. It anticipated issues that we must take seriously now and addressed them with incredible artistry. Nearly a century ago, Plečnik created a paradigm to return to, managing risk while reveling in how compelling urban life can be.

Marion Weiss is a principal at Weiss/ Manfredi and Graham Chair Professor of Architecture at the University of Pennsylvania.

→
Triple Bridge, Riverwalk, Ljubljana, Slovenia

ROME
JACK SULLIVAN

Reinvent cities through pedestrian-friendly interventions.

———

If Rome was able to become a more sustainable city, any city can change. During the Great Jubilee in 2000, there was a huge celebration, so local officials cleaned up the city and took a lot of cars off the streets, which was a big deal. They even turned the northern part of the Via del Corso into a pedestrian zone. That alone amazed me.

In 2013 Mayor Ignazio Marino closed Via dei Fori Imperiali—which leads from the Victor Emmanuel monument to the Colosseum—making it a bicycle and pedestrian zone with limited bus access. The street had been contentious ever since Mussolini rammed it through precious archaeological sites. The city finally accepted that it was totally unsustainable to let cars circle the Colosseum. We might pine for the romantic image of Audrey Hepburn and Gregory Peck doubling up on a scooter to tour the city, but we'll get over it. We'll make new memories.

Rome's car-free areas allow people to engage with each other instead of dodging motorini. These are now places where you can actually have a conversation on the street or contemplate the city's incredibly beautiful buildings. The piazza in front of the Colosseum became surprisingly quiet, and you can now hear birds. It's still a vibrant place, but without the roaring, spitting sounds and the acrid smell of engines.

Rome lost none of its charm when it changed some of its bad habits. In fact, it's more enchanting than ever. The atmosphere is safer, calmer, and more accommodating where visitors are most likely to congregate. For anyone who knew Rome in the 1970s and 1980s—like myself, for instance—the transformation is palpable and much appreciated.

The environmental benefits are clear: aside from improved sound and air quality, the city improved drainage when it reconfigured its streets for walking and biking; there are newly planted trees, but none that would block views to monuments; trucks can make deliveries at limited times of the day, so the stores and restaurants on pedestrian streets don't suffer from lack of access; and the transit system was boosted with additional bus circulation and an improved trolley line.

The city's leadership has basically rethought what Rome could be. The leadership is putting a better face on this 2,700-year-old city. The culture of the place was transformed by another cultural phenomenon: an awareness of social and environmental priorities.

Jack Sullivan is a licensed landscape architect, associate professor of landscape architecture at the University of Maryland, and fellow of the American Academy in Rome.

→

Via dei Fori Imperiali, leading to the Colosseum, Rome

SAN FRANCISCO BAY
SONJA HINRICHSEN

Use our land in a more protected way, instead of abusing it.

———

Gaspar de Portolà discovered San Francisco Bay in 1769. The map had just been a straight coastline because the first mapmakers of the west coast couldn't see the entrance to the bay from the sea. San Francisco Bay was an estuary then, rich with plant and animal life. Only 5 percent of that is left today. The rest has been eradicated by civilization.

The missionaries who came with Portolà wrote about the Ohlone tribe of Native Americans who lived there. In the missionaries' writing, the Ohlone were described as primitive because they had no permanent houses. Everything was makeshift. They didn't need much and didn't even practice agriculture. They lived off the land.

By the 1960s, when so little of the original ecosystem was left, the prognosis was that the bay would be totally filled in by 2020, with only a shipping channel left. Filling in parts of the bay had started in the 1800s. The San Francisco Marina was made of landfill, as was Treasure Island, which previously was used by the military.

The idea to fill the bay was completely reversed by an organization called Save the Bay, founded in 1961 by three women—Kay Kerr, Sylvia McLaughlin, and Esther Gulick. Their goal was to revive the bay and make it as clean and natural as possible, which was very difficult; for decades industries had been pouring oil and chemicals into it, and waste facilities had been routinely dumping trash into it.

Bit by bit, waste deposit into the bay was stopped. With the creation of the Golden Gate National Recreation Area, run by the National Park Service, much of the bay shoreline is now preserved. Some estuaries have been re-created, and natural habitats have been reestablished.

The first time I visited Crissy Field, a part of San Francisco Bay, in the late 1980s, it was an inaccessible, fenced-off military wasteland. Now it's one of the most popular and beautiful recreation sites along the shoreline.

The protection and restoration of San Francisco Bay gives me hope because this could happen everywhere. Former military and waste sites can be brought back. We can reestablish the original ecosystem, but perhaps not in its original state. We can use our land in a more protected way, instead of abusing it.

Sonja Hinrichsen is an artist whose immersive video installations and interventions examine urban and natural environments through exploration and research.

→

San Francisco Bay, California

THE SAND ENGINE
KRISTINA HILL

Learn patience and flexibility.

———

The Sand Engine, completed in the fall of 2012 near The Hague in the Netherlands, is a pilot project that, if it succeeds, will transform the management of the Dutch coast and pave the way for how to adapt to rising sea levels.

The Sand Engine is a 27.5-million-cubic-yard (21 million cu. m) sand pit that was added to the Dutch coast by dredge boats. Its purpose is to change over time, as waves and wind redistribute the sand along nine to twelve miles of coastline, forming widened beaches and higher dunes.

This method of protecting the coast was implemented at 25 percent the cost of nourishing that much shoreline with dredged sand using traditional means. The savings came from placing a higher percentage of the sand in deeper water and not paying for labor to bulldoze the sand up and down the coast and on to dune forms.

Eliminating ubiquitous annual bulldozer action provides sandy-coast ecosystems a chance to become established. Nests can survive, allowing eggs to survive and hatch; plants can germinate and grow; and unusual or suppressed populations of insects, birds, and crustaceans can rebound, linked to each other by the beach's food web.

This new shore-building approach represents the commitment of engineers and landscape architects to emulate the sand additions to the coast that were associated with glacial action for two million years, but that no longer occur.

The sand that erodes will eventually move offshore and be dredged again in a permanent, Sisyphean cycle of human action, showing that an active human role is needed to adapt to a changing climate.

This new approach also offers a model of celebrating the beauty of change. The Sand Engine allows people who visit it to witness the change over time and accept our human inability to impose a steady state on processes beyond our control.

The Sand Engine has also created one of the best point breaks for surfing in Europe. Surfing is an apt metaphor for adaptation to climatic and economic changes. We can learn patience and flexibility, to accept the poignancy of change in a dynamic environment and find it beautiful.

And we can expand both our compassion and our courage to invest our shared resources to support the human and nonhuman communities in which we exist.

Kristina Hill is professor of landscape architecture at the University of California, Berkeley.

↗
Zandmotor, Rijkwaterstaat, The Netherlands

SCHIEBLOCK
TRACY METZ

Take your city into your own hands.

———

The Dutch city of Rotterdam was bombed to smithereens by the Germans in 1940 at the beginning of World War II. The city now has the most American-looking downtown in the Netherlands, with broad, busy roads lined with chunky, uninviting, and unloved office blocks, many of which now stand empty.

Enter ZUS, the architectural practice of Kristian Koreman and Elma van Boxel. The name is an acronym for Zones Urbaines Sensibles, a politically correct French word for "sensitive urban zones," for example, ghettos.

ZUS believes in architectural activism, not in waiting around for developers to come back and save the city; the financial crisis put an end to that, and maybe these developers' ideas weren't that good anyway. So in 2001 ZUS moved into a big office building called the Schieblock—on what used to be the street with the highest number of shootings in Rotterdam—and with boundless energy and optimism, started redeveloping the area.

The transformation of both the building and its surroundings was impressive. The huge open-floor plans of the offices have been turned into spaces suitable for one-to-two-person creative companies. The ground floor houses a shop where Rotterdam's designers sell their work and a company that organizes architectural tours. The roof is a full-fledged urban vegetable garden.

It wasn't just a building that Koreman and van Boxel were aiming to revitalize. It was the neighborhood. So they set out to connect the building to its surroundings with a "Luchtsingel," an elevated bridge. With a crowd-funding campaign, they "sold" seventeen thousand wooden planks at thirty-three U.S. dollars (twenty-five euros) each. This bright yellow piece of unusual infrastructure spans not only the busy road next to the Schieblock but also the adjacent railroad tracks, and connects the building to the top of a former rail viaduct where a temporary theater has been built.

The future of Schieblock and the Luchtsingel Bridge are uncertain; there is no guarantee that ZUS's urban politics will pay off in the long run. In one sense, though, they have already paid off: they have shown what we can do when we take our city into our own hands.

Tracy Metz is a journalist and author based in Amsterdam. She is an international correspondent for Architectural Record, *a visiting fellow at Harvard's GSD, and director of the John Adams Institute.*

→

Schieblock and the Luchtsingel Bridge, Rotterdam, the Netherlands

SERENBE
MARINA KHOURY

Incorporate agriculture absolutely and completely into a community.

———

Serenbe, a community about thirty miles from Atlanta, inspires me. Serenbe is around one thousand acres, of which 70 percent is open space preserved in perpetuity. It's a unique agricultural community.

In the early 2000s the community banded together to protect farmland and prevent sprawl from encroaching on its land. People wanted to preserve the farmland, but were also open to more beautiful and sustainable growth. They realized that they couldn't say no to growth, but they wondered: how should it happen?

Agriculture is woven into the town's fabric at many scales. It's not a matter of town at one end and agriculture at the other; most lots have the town on one side and open space on another. Everyone is just a few minutes' walk to large expanses of open space.

Serenbe is principally designed as a series of hamlets or villages that have energy-efficient buildings. Typically, the buildings are one block thick and transect-based, meaning that larger lots are at the periphery and the blocks become tighter as you move into the center. The neighborhoods are walkable.

Local restaurants are farm-to-table. Community-supported agriculture is available. Waste is recycled or composted. Landscaping is native and organic. Storm water is handled carefully for the lowest impact.

And the town has these beautiful lampposts, trash cans, and benches. The people realized that arts and culture are central to their lives, and they have established an identity based on this. You know that you are in Serenbe when you see the art.

Agriculture is introduced as an amenity. The town goes beyond the saying "agriculture is the new golf" to make its farmland an asset. Everyone is invited to reconnect with the land. People can participate in food making. Kids know where their food comes from.

As more and more communities worry about the quality and cost of their food—with the latest recall or farmer's riot in the news all the time—Serenbe shows how people can sustainably bring the production, distribution, and celebration of food into their community.

Serenbe is now an example for other communities on how to find ways to legalize different scales of food production and create new codes for urban agriculture. And Serenbe can be used to further develop the planning of other agrarian communities.

This place is a model for how to incorporate agriculture absolutely and completely into a community.

Marina Khoury is a partner at Duany Plater-Zyberk & Company and manages its Washington, D.C., area office.

→
Serenbe, Georgia

SEVEN DIALS
VICTOR DOVER

Show how cool it can be to live in the city.

———

Revitalized historical places are emblematic of a sustainable future. It's been said that "the greenest building is the one that has already been built," when considering the embodied energy in the materials that we'd otherwise have to ship, throw away, or reuse in the structure.

The preservation movement began around the idea of protecting places because they are rich in character. We develop attachments to places because of their architecture and feeling, not from their machinery. Historical buildings tend to be low-tech but often feature a smart use of resources. For example, those old thick walls have thermal mass, which helps the building stay cooler on summer days and warmer on winter nights.

Old buildings often have a great building-to-street relationship, too. Their fronts—doors, windows, storefronts, balconies—face the street and the public.

Seven Dials in London is a curious intersection not far from Covent Garden. In the 1600s the developer built it with diagonal streets, which, in plan, vaguely resemble the Union Jack. At the center, the diagonal roads converge, intersecting in a square with a column in the middle.

There are no signature works of architecture around it, and the column is very simple, but there's a bench at its base, where people gather. There's something about the size, proportion, and pace of the space; people love being there. The scale feels comfortable, and the intersection slows everyone down. You can watch the human parade go by, on foot, on bikes, in cars.

Seven Dials is preserved as a national heritage site, and as is often the case, historic preservation points the way. If we had more places like it, people wouldn't need to feel like they're stuck in their cars. If people felt that good in every city, we'd have a stronger, smarter planet. Once you see the place, you know ideas fly back and forth there.

Seven Dials makes the city a place where you want to be. One no longer needs to retreat from the city to hide in backyards in the exurbs or little houses on the prairie. With this kind of urban living, there are fewer burdens on the planet because there's no impulse to flee. With more places like Seven Dials, more forests and farmland would be saved.

As Parris Glendening, former governor of Maryland, once said, "People hate sprawl, but they hate density more." But that's exactly what we need if we are going to create a sustainable future. We need more places that show how cool it can be to live in the city.

Victor Dover is a planner and principal at Dover, Kohl & Partners.

→

Seven Dials, London

SHERBOURNE COMMONS
CHRISTOPHER HUME

Make infrastructure that can do double duty.

———

When land is at a premium, there's not a lot of space to waste. Sherbourne Commons in Toronto shows how to use space to make infrastructure palatable. Sherbourne does double duty: it is both a new waterfront park and a water filtration plant.

For fifty to sixty years, this area of the Toronto waterfront was a wasteland. But soon, this new park will be surrounded by condos. Before, nobody wanted a water filtration plant in the neighborhood because "it smells and it's dirty." Now, people see how infrastructure can be an amenity.

Rainwater collects and drains into the park's underground filtration system, which then treats the storm water in a ground-level channel with large S-shaped, Russian Constructivist–looking sculptures. The system doesn't make the water treatment process invisible. People see the mesh and say, "What is this?" They then see how the system aerates the water as it flows through bulrushes.

For years, storm water was simply dumped into Lake Ontario. Now the water is cleaned before it goes into the lake. Sherbourne Commons also anticipates the expected increase in the neighborhood's storm water runoff over the next twenty to thirty years.

Sherbourne Commons is a model because it turned a water filtration plant into an aesthetic feature that people can use and enjoy. It's incredibly useful for the future, as it meets both the physical and psychological needs of our daily urban life.

Christopher Hume covers urban affairs for the Toronto Star *and is also the newspaper's architecture critic.*

→
Sherbourne Commons, Toronto, Canada

ℰ SIMS MUNICIPAL RECYCLING FACILITY
ROBERT M. ROGERS

**Design contributes to the future
at a small scale; use policy to scale up
the impact.**

———

The Sims Municipal Recycling Facility,
located on the Brooklyn waterfront at the
South Brooklyn Marine Terminal, collects
used plastic, glass, metal, and paper from
all over New York City. Sims, one of the
largest recyclers in the United States, then
sells the by-products all over the world.

Sims's new facility for the separation of
recyclable materials is delightfully elegant.
The project shows that a refined aesthetic
can be used to communicate ideas about
sustainability. Sustainability doesn't have
to have all this shagginess hanging out or
just be a celebrated drainage pit.

The policy aspect of this project is
important, too. For years the city had
separated garbage from the waste streams,
but then everything would end up in the
same landfill because there was no long-
term agreement with a waste management
company.

With the city's policy changes, there is
now a twenty-year contract for handling
waste, with an additional twenty-year option.
This change enabled Sims to make a conse-
quential investment in a state-of-the art
recycling facility.

The facility is also an educational tool.
You can take tours of the sifting facilities.
During the tour, you learn that the machines
that crush things are made in America and
the machines that sort are imported from
Europe. Recycled metals are shipped
overseas, but recycled glass and plastics are
mostly reused locally, in the United States.

The project is an overlap of policy change,
high-quality design, material science, and
sensible transportation. Because the facility is
on the waterfront, recycled materials can be
moved by barge downriver, instead of hauled
by tens of thousands of trucks over the
Verrazano Bridge.

Design professionals make contributions
to the future at a small scale; policy changes
make solutions scalable and create conse-
quential impact. The Sims facility helps
us cross boundaries and make the leap into
a sustainable future.

*Robert M. Rogers is an architect and
founding partner of Rogers Partners.*

→
Sims Municipal Recycling Facility,
Brooklyn, New York

SOLAR ROADWAYS
CHRISTOPH GIELEN

Design a new transportation system that the public can love.

———

To reduce carbon emissions, we must make improvements in our infrastructure and change our transportation habits. We need new multifunctional systems that the public can love in order to transcend political impasses.

The Solar Roadways campaign of the engineers Scott and Julie Brusaw may be just that! The duo creates solar-powered panels that can be used as building blocks for a smart road. The public response to this unusual innovation has been remarkable.

All manner of roads, driveways, and parking lots could be replaced with solar panels that can be driven on. A solar road produces electricity through photovoltaic cells underneath a heavy-duty, recycled glass surface that is shatter-resistant; its manufacture is based on airplane black box technology.

The roadway would produce renewable energy for nearby homes or feed into the electrical grid. Embedded LED lights could prevent accidents by signaling cars about oncoming obstacles. The panels would even have the ability to heat the street surface to just above freezing, so drivers would no longer have to worry about snow and ice in wintertime. The roadway would be able to monitor its own conditions. Communication lines could be run through the roads, replacing conventional ones above ground. And in the far future, the roadway could power autonomous vehicles.

We have about thirty thousand square miles of road space that could be transformed with Solar Roadways technology, but at what cost? A complete cost analysis hasn't been published as of June 2014, but the consensus among journalists is that installation costs might be 50 percent to 300 percent higher than building a regular road. Each twelve-square-foot (3.6 sq. m) panel may cost around ten thousand dollars, or four million dollars per mile. A one-mile-stretch (1.6 km) would take twenty years to pay for itself, at 2010 energy prices, with the amount of energy that it creates over that time.

It is important to recall that ambitious U.S. public works have been successfully funded before. In the 1950s the Federal Highway Administration spent twenty-five billion dollars over ten years to build up the national highway system and recouped all costs by taxes on fuel. And the Federal Highway Administration recently provided funding for building a Solar Roadways prototype—a parking lot with all these features, which is now complete.

People are eager for sustainable solutions—let's start by implementing Solar Roadways parking lots.

Christoph Gielen is an aerial photographer and author of the recent book Ciphers.

↗
Solar Roadways pilot

STELLAR APARTMENTS
KATRIN KLINGENBERG

Boost the efficiency of multifamily housing with passive house design.
_____

Stellar Apartments in Eugene, Oregon—designed by the architects Jan Fillinger and Win Swafford—is the first certified, multifamily passive house project in the United States.

Energy efficiency is at the core of sustainability. The passive house movement in the United States and elsewhere is about reducing energy consumption in buildings through reasonable ways so it doesn't cost an arm and a leg. Passive principles are about comfort and health, too.

Passive houses are not new, and the concept was not created in Germany, despite popular opinion. The U.S. Department of Energy financed some of the first models in the 1970s and 1980s.

Passive houses have continuous insulation; a thermal bridge–free design; a durable, airtight envelope; good hydrothermal performance, meaning that they don't allow any condensation in the walls that could result in mold; and high-performing windows. They also optimize solar orientation, with the right amount of solar gain achieved through correctly siting the house.

After incorporating all these elements, passive houses need ventilation. They have heat recovery ventilation systems that ensure superior indoor air freshness at all times by addressing health issues like the volatile organic compounds (VOCs) released from furniture and building materials. Basically, passive houses are always ventilated even if the owner forgets to open the windows. With indoor air filters, the air is very clean.

Multifamily housing is a way to further reduce energy consumption. With the multifamily configuration, the building has a more energy-efficient volume-to-surface ratio. This is about the relationship between the building envelope and the enclosed floor area. Larger envelopes have more usable floor areas, which means less heat loss per square foot. In practice, the walls are also then much cheaper.

Many single-family passive houses have been built. Stellar Apartments, which has been certified by the Passive House Institute U.S., shows that we can become even more efficient when we build larger shells. We can also be more efficient while paying less.

Developers have started taking up this model. And if all cities used passive house standards for their retrofit programs, we'd have a realistic chance to make a dent in carbon dioxide emissions from the building sector. This has to happen in the next twenty years, or the predicted outcomes are dire.

Energy efficiency is the detail that needs to go into the green neighborhood, otherwise it's not green.

Katrin Klingenberg is executive director of the Passive House Institute U.S.

→
Stellar Apartments, Eugene, Oregon

TENNESSEE VALLEY AUTHORITY
DAVID LEVEN

Fit infrastructure into its natural setting.

———

The Tennessee Valley Authority (TVA), a Great Depression–era regional initiative centered in Tennessee but actually covering eleven states, is amazing for its integration of engineering, design, and social impact. By the 1930s much of this area of the rural south had been deforested. As a result, farming in the region—which was crushingly poor—was suffering from excessive erosion.

The TVA helped control the erosion but also started a program of modernization and energy production through a series of dams that created hydropower, and essentially helped bring rural Tennessee into the twentieth century. Today the TVA remains the largest public energy provider in the United States, maintaining hydropower dams, coal plants, and nuclear power, implementing total energy production.

While the dams were a massive engineering project, they were conceived with a real design sensibility. The TVA Office of Architecture that was responsible for all aspects of the design of the system, from the concrete surfaces to the detailing of the dams, also applied a singular design vocabulary to the residential buildings that were built to house staff, and to the design of the roads that wound through the countryside around the dams and rivers. While there was a debate about whether to use a neoclassical or a modern approach to the architecture of the buildings in the system, thankfully the latter prevailed and followed many of the concepts of modernism and the machine aesthetic that were abundant at the time.

There was a total approach to the road systems, too, which showed a real sensitivity to the land. It wasn't just about blanketing and bulldozing roads but gently setting roads into the landscape. The design was also by nature regional and holistic, from the network all the way down to the individual objects—the dams and buildings.

I have seen the dams close up while white water canoeing on the Ocoee River. They are set within beautiful rural areas, but they are highly technological. The TVA project shows how infrastructure can fit into a natural setting, in ways that are both aggressive and respectful.

David Leven is a partner at the New York-based architecture firm LEVENBETTS and associate professor in the graduate architecture program at Parsons School of Constructed Environments.

↗

Tennessee River and Tennessee Valley Authority
Chickamauga and Fontana Dams, Tennessee and
North Carolina

TERMITE MOUNDS
JANINE BENYUS

Use nature's blueprints.

———

Research is under way to examine how termites use their mounds to regulate temperature and gases without an external heating or cooling device. Scientists and architects from a number of universities are working together on this research. In one instance, they poured plaster of paris into a termite mound found in Africa to highlight all the interior fissures. Scientists then imaged the termite mound with a giant slice and scan machine, creating a layer-by-layer view. They are now reassembling the data to find the underlying design principles. And researchers are computing the mound's fluid dynamics.

Some mounds in Africa reach eight to nine feet (2.4–2.7 m) high. The mound is earth-baled and very strong but also porous. Termites don't actually live in the mound; very high numbers live underneath it, where they farm fungus. To do this, they need the temperature to remain exactly at 87 degrees Fahrenheit, no matter how cold or hot the air gets aboveground.

What researchers have discovered is that the mound functions as a lung. It regulates what levels of oxygen and carbon dioxide are needed. Air moves in and out of its channels, taking advantage of how the wind flows through the mound to create differentiated air pressures that evacuate old carbon dioxide and pull in oxygen. The porous clay contracts and expands. It is a self-regulating structure.

Dr. Scott Turner, one of the world's great termite experts at the State University of New York, is also involved in the project and says that the termite mound is an extension of the physiology of the termite colony. Natural selection also works on the design of the mound-lung.

Once we understand the designs, we can create walls in our buildings that mimic the termites' "lung": they can be porous, breathing building skins, enabling the exchange of gases.

In nature things are built from the bottom-up, just like in 3-D printing. There is no waste, unlike when we cut two-by-fours to the size we need, for instance. 3-D printing will help us get closer to how nature builds: there will be no more blocks of amorphous concrete; they will be bonelike for light-weight strength and have smart channels for airflow.

This termite project represents one of the first times that architects are getting detailed blueprints from nature. But it is just the first of many collaborations with nature's design intelligence.

Janine Benyus is founder of Biomimicry 3.8 and author of Biomimicry: Innovation Designed by Nature.

→
African termite mound

UNITÉ D'HABITATION
ANTHONY FLINT

Build efficient and affordable housing in our fast-growing cities.

———

It was pilloried even before its opening in 1952, decried by local officials as having unhealthy density, and blamed for spawning copycat versions of towers in the park and public housing blocks such as Pruitt-Igoe in St. Louis, Missouri, famously demolished as a coda of modernism. But Le Corbusier's Unité d'Habitation in Marseille, France, holds hopeful lessons for efficient housing in the fast-growing metropolitan areas of the twenty-first century.

The project was the first in the architect's Ville Radieuse scheme, with 337 compact apartments stacked in twelve stories, shops and a restaurant within, and a rooftop hosting a gymnasium, open space, and a school. The entire structure is set on thick but graceful pilotis, freeing the ground level for circulation among the parks and pathways all around.

The apartments, mostly composed of two stories with one floor running the width of the building, feature compact kitchen and dining areas, sliding walls, built-in shelving, balconies, and small rectangular bedrooms— essentially the super-efficient design found in what today is referred to as microhousing. Many elements were prefabricated to speed construction and lower costs. The idea was to pack it all in densely but to provide all the basic living space that residents need, with amenities only an elevator ride away, but also just outside the urban environment of the location.

The contemporary architect Bjarke Ingels has said that he was directly inspired by Le Corbusier's comprehensive approach and efficient housing design in such projects as the 8 House.

Le Corbusier sought to address the housing needs of France after World War II. Providing decent and affordable housing remains a top priority in burgeoning cities, particularly in the developing world, which are gaining population at a staggering pace. Elements of Unité d'Habitation would be rightly gleaned for a path to those cities' sustainable urban future.

Anthony Flint is a fellow and director of public affairs at the Lincoln Institute of Land Policy, and author of Modern Man: The Life of Le Corbusier, Architect of Tomorrow.

→

Unité d'Habitation, Marseille, France

VERNACULAR ARCHITECTURE
LI XIAODONG

Live with nature.

———

Vernacular architecture responds to the local climate and lifestyle. These buildings have always been the most sustainable throughout history and have morphed into various local forms today.

B. V. Doshi, an Indian architect, worked for Louis Kahn and Le Corbusier, two of the top modern architects. He somehow managed to adapt modern architecture for India, creating an approach acceptable to Indian conditions and climate. He understood the lifestyle of Indians.

Geoffrey Bawa in Sri Lanka also adapted contemporary architecture for local conditions, creating ingenious sustainable architecture.

What Doshi and Bawa have done—and others are now doing—gives me hope because they realize that it's about the process and not about design. Architecture should be based in a dialogue with local conditions and lifestyles. It should be a product of that dialogue, a reflection of those conditions.

This is the opposite of modern architecture, which is the idea of a few designers superimposed on a program, with an industrial process of production totally detached from place. Vernacular architecture is about an attitude of how to approach architecture: How can we sustain our culture and lifestyle? How can we live with nature?

Li Xiaodong is principal at Lixiaodong Atelier.

→
Indian Institute of Management, designed by B. V. Doshi, Bangalore, 1983

WIND MEGA COMPLEXES
LESTER BROWN

China and the United States: Move to renewable energy together.

___

What I find exciting is something that will shape our future by moving us away from a carbon-based economy—the six Wind Mega Complexes in China. Each complex has a generating capacity of at least twenty thousand megawatts. That means each complex has a generation capacity equal to twenty nuclear power plants.

The largest of the six complexes is in Inner Mongolia. It will have thirty-eight thousand megawatts of generating capacity. This one wind farm could provide for the energy needs of a country the size of Poland.

All six are now under construction. This is not someone's fantasy but a reality, something that is under way.

If China can develop wind resources on this scale, it can avoid building 120 coal-fired power plants. If China combines these wind facilities with solar power, we can begin to see how the Chinese can meet their energy needs with clean, renewable sources.

If China and the United States, the world's two largest economies, can move toward renewable energy production together, then we have a chance to reduce coal use for the world as a whole. We can then hope to prevent runaway climate change.

Lester Brown is president and founder of the Earth Policy Institute. His most recent book is Breaking New Ground.

→
China Wind Complex

IMAGE CREDITS

ACKNOWLEDGMENTS

First, thank you to all the contributors. Everyone somehow fit me into their incredibly busy schedules and was very generous with their inspirations and encouragement. If all these amazing people didn't care, this book wouldn't have happened. Thank you again for making it possible.

A special thank-you to Maria Bellalta, Suzanne Preston Blier, John Cary, Janet Echelman, Mark Focht, Christian Gabriel, Kristen Richards, Jason Schupbach, Jack Sullivan, and Yu Kongjian for their extra help.

Also, I want to thank Jennifer Lippert, Meredith Baber, Russell Fernandez, Emily Malinowski, Mia Johnson, Paul Wagner, and everyone else at Princeton Architectural Press for helping a first-time author learn the ropes. Their hard work actually made the book appear in print.

To Homer Reid, Jaime Jennings, Ben Wellington, Curt Millay, Dena Kennett, Liz Guthrie, Lindsey Milstein, Susan Cahill-Aylward, and Gretchen Ward, thank you for being ever-patient sounding boards. And to Terry Poltrack and Nancy Somerville, thank you for allowing me to do this in my free time (what's that?), alongside my work.

Thank you to my parents for buying me all those books. This book is dedicated to Laura, Audrey, and James H.